No. 1065
$15.95

Model Railroad Photography

by Paul Garrison

 TAB BOOKS Inc.
BLUE RIDGE SUMMIT, PA. 17214

FIRST EDITION

FIRST PRINTING

FEBRUARY 1981

Copyright © 1981 by TAB BOOKS Inc.

Printed in the United States of America

Library of Congress Cataloging in Publication Data

Garrison, Paul.
    Model railroad photography.

    Includes index.
    1. Photography, Table-top. 2. Railroads—Models.
I. Title.
TR683.5.G37   778.9′962519   80-20076
ISBN 0-8306-9924-4
ISBN 0-8306-1065-0 (pbk.)

Contents

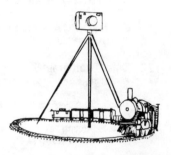

Preface

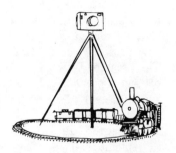

Model railroaders come in many stripes. Some like to build huge complicated layouts on which two, three or more trains can be operated simultaneously according to carefully prepared schedules. Others like to play with electronic problems, often resulting in fully automated operation, with the moving train setting its own switches, activating signal lights and the like. Still others may prefer to spend their time building engines and rolling stock from scratch or modifying and super detailing commercially available kits. And then there are those to whom the realism of the miniature landscape is more important than the running of trains.

No matter what the modeler's individual preference might be, sooner or later he is likely to find that he would like to produce a photographic record of his work, either to simply own such photographs as a permanent record of his accomplishment, or possibly in order to illustrate a story which he may want to submit to one of the model railroad magazines.

Probably the most famous among model railroaders who successfully combined photography and model rail-roading was the late John Allen, whose Gorre & Daphetid railroad layout was the subject of a great many articles in the *Model Railroader* and the *Railroad Model Craftsman*. John was a photographer to start with and, as a result, whatever he built he did so with an eye toward effective photography. The fact that his was a very large and complicated operating layout simply meant that his overriding interest in photography did not prevent him from also wanting a layout which actually worked.

The fact is that, unless the problems associated with being able to take exciting pictures are taken into consideration from the very beginning, it often proves difficult if not actually impossible to end up with anything more exciting than a series of rather dull snapshots.

When we talk about photographs of model railroads they must necessarily fall into several different categories. There are long shots of the entire layout in which it is virtually always quite obvious that we are looking at a model rather than the real thing. The point of view, more often than not, resembles an aerial photograph, and the value of such a picture is primarily that it shows the work as a whole. When intelligently lit, such images need not necessarily be dull, but their impact is usually restricted to showing the size and intricacy of the model.

Another category consists of close-ups of a particular subject, such as a building, an engine, one or several cars, or an intricate piece of landscaping. Here we are concerned with showing every bit of detail as clearly as possible to impress the viewer with the amount of expert workmanship which went into the construction of the model. Such photographs are often best taken not on the actual layout, but either against a plain background, or in a small setting created specifically for the purpose of obtaining the desired result.

The third, and, to me, the most exciting type of photograph is the scene which makes a small portion of the layout appear as if it was photographed outdoors on an actual railroad setting. Here individual details are less important than the overall effect, and camera angle and lighting play an important part.

The camera angle is so important that we'll look at its effect in considerable detail in several chapters in this book. Quite obviously, the camera lens should be in a position which coincides with a place where a person could logically be expected to be standing in order to take that picture, if the subject were the real thing rather than a model. And cameras, even 35-mm cameras, are bulky and clumsy in relation to the subject being photographed, making it frequently difficult to find the right place to put them.

Lighting also plays an important part. Are we looking for a midday effect when the light is relatively flat and there are few shadows, or would we prefer the scene to look like early morning or dusk? Virtually all actual railroad scenes are outdoors, meaning that the light is produced by a single source, the sun. Thus, our lighting should also give the impression that it emanates from a single source, with all shadows falling in the same direction.

It might be said here that a modeler, whose primary interest is to create great photographic images of his work, may find that he never gets around to actually building a working layout. What he may end up with is a multitude of small scenes in which the railroad is a major or minor part of the landscape and, unless he feels otherwise inclined, he may never actually electrify the rails for operation.

Most of the photographs in this book were taken on several different layouts which I have built over the years in a series of apartments and houses in which I have lived. All of these layouts were in N-gauge. N-gauge means that the scale is 160:1. In other words, something that measures 13 feet 4.3 inches in real life will measure one inch in N-gauge. Photographing models built in such a small scale results in greater physical difficulties than would be encountered if the models were in a larger scale, such as HO (87:1), S (64:1) or 0-gauge (48:1). But since I like my layouts to actually work, and since space has always been at a premium, I decided to opt for the smaller scale and accept the added difficulties involved in getting good pictures.

I might state right here that I don't consider myself to be an expert modeler, on par with those who habitually walk away with prizes at the annual convention of the National Model Railroad Association (NMRA). My model work is designed to please me and nobody else. Therefore, in examining the illustrations in this book, you will find that I have used many commercially available kit-built structures, though most have been modified in one way or another. Also, all the rolling stock was purchased off the shelf. I am pointing this out because what I was after were the photographic effects rather than to prove some sort of great talent in making the most perfect possible models.

So, now let's get down to business.

Paul Garrison

Chapter 1
Photographic
Equipment

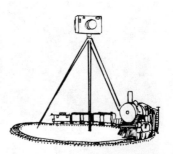

All the photographs reproduced in this book were taken with a 35-mm Canon single lens reflex camera. The lenses used were either a 50-mm normal, a 28-mm wide angle, or a 100-200-mm zoom lens, and many excellent effects were achieved by attaching one, two or three close-up lenses to the front of the 50-mm lens (Fig. 1-1).

While Edward Steichen, probably one of the greatest photographers ever, used to say that a good photographer can produce an exciting photograph with a pin-hole camera as well as with the most expensive equipment available, this does not hold true when we're trying to take pictures of our model railroad. While the particular make and type of camera is of no great consequence, it must have certain capabilities which are not available with all cameras.

CAMERA REQUIREMENTS

Above all, the camera must be capable of accepting a variety of lenses. Any camera with only one fixed lens will necessarily result in restrictions which will make it impossible to obtain some of the more intricate images. Second, double-lens reflex cameras of the Rolleiflex type are difficult to use because, with the subject nearly always being just inches from the lens, the parallax problem becomes nearly insurmountable. Also, the instant-print cameras, like the ones manufactured by Polaroid or Eastman Kodak, do not lend themselves to this kind of photography because they're too

Fig. 1-1. All photos in the book were taken by the author with a 35mm single lens reflex camera, as shown here equipped with a 50mm normal lens. Also shown alongside are #1, #2, and #3 close-up lenses.

big, and the picture being propelled out of the bottom of the camera would, most likely, end up pushing the subject being photographed out of the way. Sheet-film cameras in which the focusing is done on a ground glass would be ideal, except again, for their awkward size.

Fig. 1-2. A cable release with a hold-screw makes steady time exposures possible.

Fig. 1-3. In this photograph we look down from the top at the scene which was set up to illustrate the effects of different lenses and f-stops.

Fig. 1-4. This picture was taken from a distance of 8.5 inches from the in-focus train, using a 28mm lens, wide open.

Fig. 1-5. Here the identical set-up was used, but the lens was stopped down to f/16.

Fig. 1-6. Here we used a 50mm lens, wide open, with the camera 18 inches from the in-focus train.

Fig. 1-7. The same set-up, but with the lens stopped down to f/16.

Fig. 1-8. Here we have added the #1 close-up lens to the 50mm lens, used wide open. Camera-to-subject distance was 12.75 inches.

Fig. 1-9. The same, stopped down to f/16.

Fig. 1-10. Now we are using #1 and #2 close-up lenses in conjunction with the 50mm lens, wide open, at a distance of 8 inches.

Fig. 1-11. The same at f/16.

Fig. 1-12. Now we have added the #3 close-up lens to the above. Used wide open at a distance of 5 inches.

Fig. 1-13. The same at f/16.

Fig. 1-14. Again the combination of a 50mm lens with #1, 2 and 3 close-up lenses, wide open at 5 inches.

Fig. 1-15. The same at f/16.

Fig. 1-16. This was shot using the zoom lens set to 100mm, wide open, at a distance of 8 feet.

Fig. 1-17. The same, stopped down to f/16.

Fig. 1-18. Without moving the camera, we changed the zoom position to 200mm, using it wide open.

Fig. 1-19. The same at f/16.

Fig. 1-20. Here the 50mm lens with all three close-up lenses was used, wide open.

Fig. 1-21. The same at f/8.

Fig. 1-22. The same at f/16.

Fig. 1-23. A 28mm lens was used, 16 inches from the subject, stopped down to f/16.

Fig. 1-24. The same at f/11.

Fig. 1-25. The same at f/8.

This tends to bring us back to the 35-mm single lens reflex cameras which are small in size and with which there is no parallax problem. Looking at the scene through the viewer shows us exactly what we can expect to get on the film.

OTHER EQUIPMENT

And that brings us to the other piece of equipment which is an absolute necessity, namely a good tripod. Many of the exposures

Fig. 1-26. The same at f/566.

Fig. 1-27. The same at f/2.8.

may have to be too long to permit hand holding the camera. We must have a steady tripod and the camera must be able to be operated with a cable release (Fig. 1-2) instead of the usual

Fig. 1-28. Now we have moved the camera to within 5 inches of the subject, using the 50mm lens with the three close-up lenses. Stop: f/1.8.

Fig. 1-29. The same at f/4.

exposure button. No matter how steady the tripod, pushing a button will cause it to move. Only a cable release makes it possible to get perfectly steady time exposures.

Fig. 1-30. The same at f/8.

Fig. 1-31. The same at f/16.

There's one additional gadget that often comes in handy. It's an offset bracket which is mounted on the tripod and on which the camera can be mounted, ending up cantilevered several inches from the top of the tripod itself. If such a bracket of adequate length is not available at the local camera shop, it can be made to order by any halfway decently equipped machine shop. The advantage with such a gadget is, it is possible to firmly place the camera in a position on the layout, where a tripod cannot be put. It may, of course, become practically impossible to look through the viewer, but that's a problem we'll get to later on.

What follows here (Figs. 1-3 through 1-31) are several series of photographs in which the same subject has been photographed, using different lenses and different f-stops. These photographs graphically illustrate the effects which can be obtained using the lenses and equipment described in this chapter.

Chapter 2
Composition
And Lighting

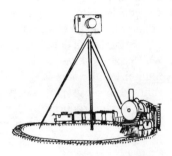

Effective photographs are distinguished by two primary parameters: composition and lighting. Composition, the art of cropping a picture for maximum pictorial impact (Fig. 2-1), is a matter of taste and of the photographer's ability to look at a subject and to visualize it within the framework of a given proportion.

FRAMING

While it is always possible to shoot a picture and then crop it afterwards to achieve a desired framing (Fig. 2-2), this is not too practical when working with 35-mm film, because what's left usually ends up being simply too small.

This is not too serious when we are working in black and white (or with color negative film), because in making the prints we can blow up the desired portion of the negative image, and with modern film, graininess is no longer a serious problem.

On the other hand, when we're using film which results in 35-mm color transparencies (slides), then any amount of cropping would mean that the resulting picture turns out to be too small to be viewed without a magnifying glass or by projection. It is therefore considerably more satisfactory if the cameraman takes the pain and time to frame the picture as correctly as possible in the view finder.

LIMITING SUBJECT MATTER

A mistake which is frequently made by photographers is the attempt to include too much in one picture as is shown in Fig. 2-3.

In most instances less is more, meaning that the final picture should concentrate on one primary object, as in Fig. 2-4, not a whole bunch of them. This one object, whatever it might be, especially in relation to model railroading, will usually be enhanced by some foreground detail and by a background which enhances the scene rather than detracting from it. While it is usually quite acceptable to let the background go out of focus, the foreground detail is in most instances better kept in sharp focus.

Foreground detail lends depth to the picture (Fig. 2-5), depth which can be exaggerated by using short-focal-length lenses or minimized by using long-focal-length lenses. In terms of model-railroad photography we will usually find that the increased perspective produced by short-focal-length wide-angle lenses is preferable (See Fig. 2-6), because it causes small areas to appear more spacious.

LIGHTING FOR EFFECT

While composition, being largely a matter of individual taste, cannot really be taught, lighting is a different matter. Lighting is the very basis of photography and, since in photographing our

Fig. 2-1. Here is a print of a full negative which should be cropped as shown in order to eliminate most of the out-of-focus rocks in the foreground and that bit of mess in the upper right-hand corner.

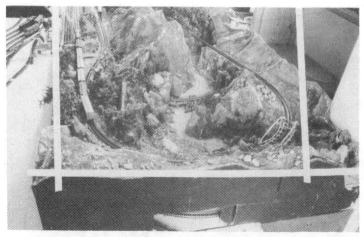

Fig. 2-2. In this scene, cropping away the unfinished portion of scenery at the right greatly improves the picture.

model railroad we have complete control over the type of lighting we use, it is up to us to create the kind of effect we are after.

Basically photographic lighting should consist of one primary light source, the so-called key light, plus whatever amount of fill-in light is needed in order to retain the appropriate amount of detail in the shadow areas. One key light alone, except when placed quite near the camera, will usually result in excessive contrast, with detail in both the highlights and the shadows likely to be lost (Fig. 2-7).

Let's always remember that model-railroad scenes are nearly always ostensibly outdoor scenes. In other words, the picture should look as if it were illuminated by the sun (or moon). A key light at a high overhead position will give the impression of midday. The lower the position of the key light and the greater the angle at which it points toward the subject, the earlier or later in the day the picture will appear to have been taken. In addition, the strong highlights and long shadows resulting from low-angle lighting tend to add considerable drama to the picture.

In Figs. 2-8 through 2-14, I have used lighting in a number of different ways on the same scene to illustrate different effects as described above.

THE COLOR OF LIGHT

Except when looking at a sunrise or sunset, we are rarely aware of the difference in the color of light by which our

25

Fig. 2-3. Many photographers tend to want to include too much detail in the same picture.

surroundings are illuminated. But there is, in fact, a considerable difference in the color of daylight during different times of the day, and on clear days in contrast to days with a solid overcast. And the artificial light we use, incandescent or fluorescent, varies in color. All these differences are greatly exaggerated on color film. Most of the color film we use is designed to give a relatively true color rendition under average daylight.

Fig. 2-4. It is better if a picture concentrates on one single subject.

"White" Daylight

There is no point here to go into detail with reference to the scientific analysis of light in terms of wavelengths, temperature and so on. Suffice it to say that we expect daylight to be white

Fig. 2-5. Foreground detail lends depth to a picture.

Fig. 2-6. Short-focal-length lenses create the impression of greater distance.

(colorless) and our brain automatically makes the necessary adjustment to cause us to see artificial light also as white, though, in fact, it is not. Moonlight, on the other hand, we see as somewhat bluish, thinking of it as "cold" light.

Fig. 2-7. A single key light without fill-in will result in excessive contrast and loss of detail in the shadows and highlights.

28

Fig. 2-8. With the key light near the camera we achieve flat lighting and little depth effect.

Fig. 2-9. Using the same flat lighting but making the background lighter improves the effect somewhat.

Fig. 2-10. Moving the light farther to the right of the camera starts to bring out the surface detail.

Fig. 2-11. Moving the key light to a far left and low position gives the impression of morning or evening, and further sharpens the surface detail.

But film has no brain to make those automatic adjustments. It sees light as it is in relation to the kind of light for which the emulsion was designed. Thus, when we expose daylight film with artificial light it will produce a yellow-orange image. Conversely, when we expose film designed for artificial light with day-light, it will produce a bluish image.

Fig. 2-12. Moving it still farther forward increases that effect.

Fig. 2-13. Now it is night, the building being apparently lit by some off-scene street lamp.

Light from a flash unit is relatively close in color to daylight and will produce an acceptable color rendition on day-light film. But I never use flash light because I prefer to be able to study the direction and intensity of the light with my eyes, something which is not possible when using flash.

Fig. 2-14. Here the effect is that all the light emanates from the building itself. No key light was used, but reflected light from a white cardboard provided the needed outside illumination.

Interesting effects can be achieved by mixing different colors of light. Say, we want to get the effect of early dawn or late dusk. By illuminating the entire scene with a fairly weak bluish light, either diffused daylight or artificial photographic lights with a light blue gelatin filter (80C), and by then adding one artificial light source without filter at a low angle, we'll be able to come up with a very exciting mixture of light reminiscent of sunrise or sunset.

"Blue" Nightlight

For a night scene, assuming we want to give the impression of a full moon, we might cover our light source with a somewhat darker blue gelatin filter (80A), giving the entire scene a bluish tint, which will be greatly enhanced if we have lights on the scene being photographed, such as locomotive headlights, lights in the windows of buildings, pasenger cars or cabooses, signals, street-lights and the like. All the these will be quite yellow, giving a realistic night effect.

As is true with virtually everything else in photography, a bit of experimentation will show what works well and what doesn't. Never hesitate to try something, no matter how unorthodox. It may just result in a stunning picture.

Chapter 3
The Layout

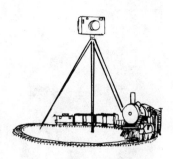

Model railroaders build layouts in every conceivable shape and size, both, more often than not, dictated by the available space. Relatively simple small layouts may be built on a four-by-eight-foot piece of plywood, and placed away from the walls to permit access from all four sides. Others may be constructed on a base of wooden grids, often extending along two or three walls (Fig. 3-1). Still others, also usually constructed on such a system of grids, cover huge areas, requiring cunningly concealed access holes to permit the modeler to reach hard-to-get-at places.

PLAN FOR CAMERA ACCESS

What few builders of such layouts will consider when they first start to plan them, is whether or not it will be possible to get at most or all portions of the layout with a camera. Even those access holes in large layouts are usually designed with the thought in mind that the operator can use the full length of his arm, an average of two to two-and-a-half feet, in order to reach whatever he needs to get at. But a camera is different. Not only does it need to be placed on a tripod, but it also must be able to get its lens close to the subject to be photographed, and there must be room for the photographer to get his head close to the viewfinder.

CONSIDER THE BACKGROUND

And there is also the question about background. If the layout is of the island type, meaning that it is placed away from the walls, it will either be necessary to construct some sort of background

33

Fig. 3-1. Layouts can be constructed to fit along several walls of a room. This permits large layouts with relatively little width, which later on simplifies the task of photographing them.

Fig. 3-2. Windows or other room features are unacceptable in the background of a picture.

Fig. 3-3. A high mountain range in the center of an island layout can effectively serve as a background, no matter from which direction the photograph is taken.

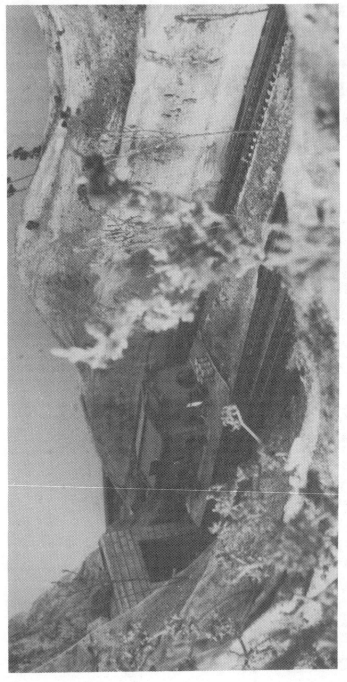

Fig. 3-4. A plain wall can serve as a background, assuming we manage to avoid getting shadows on it.

each time photographs are to be taken in order to avoid having a background full of windows, doors, and pictures on the walls (as in Fig. 3-2), or the center of the layout should consist of a high mountain range which would then act as background, no matter from which side of the layout the picture is to be taken (Fig. 3-3).

If the layout is built against a plain wall, it can usually serve quite satisfactorily as a background (Fig. 3-4), though it is sometimes difficult to avoid getting shadows on it. And, after all, who ever heard of a shadow on the sky? Personally I have found that, whenever possible, I prefer to have some part of the actual layout, a mountain, building or the like, be the background. Some modelers go to great lengths to paint a huge picture of an appropriate landscape to be used as a background. Depending on

Fig. 3-5. Mountain scenery, in addition to providing effective backgrounds, makes it possible to hide the trackwork of return loops.

Fig. 3-6. Here the track disappears behind a mountain.

the talent as a painter, this can be quite effective. The trouble is, I can't paint worth a darn, and though I do have some scenic photographs which would do the trick, making color blowups of the appropriate size could run into many hundreds if not thousands of dollars. Wherever possible I therefore prefer to have mountains rise against the wall, thus providing an integral three-dimensional background.

As the reader may have noticed in the different photographs in this book, I am prone to include a lot of mountain scenery. The reasons are twofold. One is the fact that I live in Santa Fe, surrounded by all manner of tall mountains, and this is the type of country I happen to like best. The other is that it permits hiding portions of the trackwork, such as those unrealistic return loops, behind and under mountains (Figs. 3-5 and 3-6), creating a multitude of operational possibilities without having the whole thing end up looking ridiculous.

One of the most photogenic layouts I ever built was a U-shaped around-the-walls affair seen during its early stages of construction in Fig. 3-1. It was fairly narrow with some bulges on the ends to permit return loops without excessively tight curves. The total length of the three sides of the U was approximately thirty feet, and about 90 percent of the whole layout was easily accessible for photography. This was enhanced by the fact that I tried to build most of the more interesting scenic effects as close to the edge of the layout as possible to permit shooting extreme closeups with the least amount of complication.

Chapter 4
Scenery

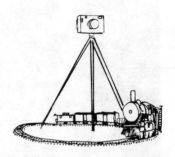

Scenery is to model railroading what butter (or margarine) is to bread. Without butter, bread is nourishing but dull. Without scenery as shown in Fig. 4-1, a railroad may run just fine, but it's dull. As a result, in the best photographs the trains and the track are just incidental. It is the surrounding detail (Fig. 4-2) that makes the picture.

There is no accepted right or wrong way to go about creating scenery for model railroads. Virtually every modeler will devise some methods which work for him while they may be shunned by others. For the purposes of this book, then, let me briefly describe my own methods, primarily because the results are what we see in all the photographs in this book.

TRACKWORK

I have to admit that I'm a bit sloppy about my trackwork. Building a raised ballast base (Fig. 4-3) for the track always seems like more work than it is worth. So I usually simply tack ready-made bendable track on top of whatever base I am using for that particular portion of the layout (Fig. 4-4).

I know that there are some modelers who go to the extreme of actually laying each individual tie. The result is by far superior to anything I have ever done, but maybe those people simply have more time than I available for their modeling work. Personally I would rather spend my time in creating and building scenic effects

Fig. 4-1. Without scenery a layout is dull.

than to put dozens, if not hundreds, of hours into fooling around with the trackwork itself. Admittedly, it shows in some of the photographs, but most of the time I have been able to satisfactorily disguise it by simply spreading some scale ballast around the tracks. The only thing that concerns me about the track is that it is capable of supporting trains without an unnecessary number of derailments. Therefore, those among the readers who are purists, please don't look at the trackwork in the photographs. I know that isn't up to your standards. But it worked and gave me many hours of pleasure. And, after all, giving pleasure is what the hobby is all about.

TOPOGRAPHY

One of the first considerations that affect the planning of a new layout is the topography of the country in which it is supposed to be operating (Fig. 4-5). To put it as simply as possible, there are four choices—flat country, like Kansas or some of the surrounding plains states, rolling hills, such as may be found in northern New

Fig. 4-2. The scenic detail surrounding the track is what makes the picture.

Jersey or upstate New York, —real mountains as are everywhere in the Rocky Mountain states, or, if we are talking about a traction layout, a city.

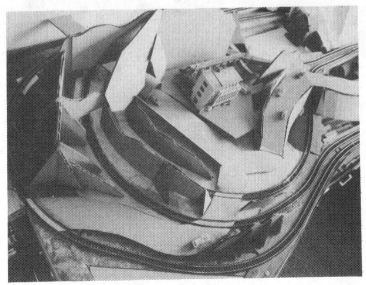

Fig. 4-3. Building a raised ballast base for the track always seems to me to be more work than it is worth.

41

Fig. 4-4. I always use ready-made bendable track.

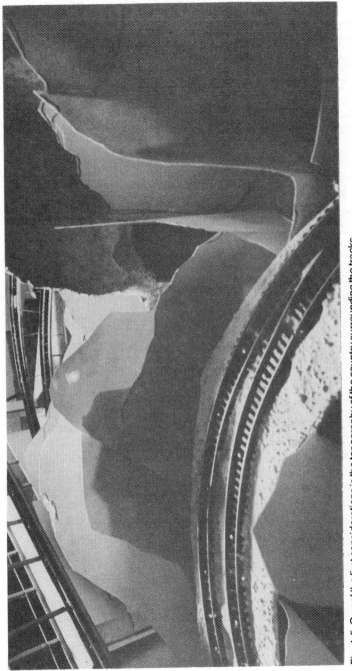

Fig. 4-5. One of the first considerations is the topography of the country surrounding the tracks.

Fig. 4-6. Some layouts are built on a solid surface, such as a piece of plywood.

MOUNTAINS

Personally, I have always been partial to the Rocky Mountain type of landscape (which is why I am living in Santa Fe) because it is not only the most spectacular, but it also permits all kinds of convoluted trackwork in a relatively small area, some of which can then be hidden behind all those mountains. So, let's talk about a mountain topography, which is really the only type I know anything about.

Envision The Area

Regardless of whether the layout in its entirety is built on a solid surface, such as a sheet of plywood (Fig. 4-6) or of composition board, I generally start by envisioning what seems to me to be a logical, if somewhat compressed, group of mountains and valleys, with possibly a river running through one of those valleys. The riverbed, then, is the lowest elevation anywhere on the layout, and anything else has to be built up from that level. The next step is to scrounge a bunch of old cartons which can usually be found at any supermarket or liquor store. The corrugated cardboard contained in those cartons is what I use to construct what I refer to as the armature for the topography (Fig. 4-7). In other words, what I do is to cut hundreds of "ribs" which I glue vertically onto the layout base (Fig. 4-8). These ribs represent the vertical profile of the various parts of the topography I am trying to create. Once one particular section of the layout has been so "ribbed" (Fig. 4-9) it is time for the next step.

Fig. 4-7. Corrugated cardboard is cut from cartons to be used for the ribs which are the skeleton of the future landscape.

Cover the "Ribs"

The next step involves placing a covering over those ribs. For this I use cheesecloth. I smear a liberal amount of rubber cement onto the top edges of the ribs and then stretch cheesecloth across them, creating a more or less continuous surface. Since rubber cement takes a while to really dry, it is usually a good idea to wait until the next day to start with the following step.

Apply Plaster

That next step requires a fairly thin mixture of patching plaster (or any kind of plaster) and water. This mixture is applied to the cheesecloth with a brush. A bit of trial and error will determine how thin the mixture should be. It must be thin enough to be easily spreadable but not so watery that it drips through the cheesecloth. Once all parts of the cheesecloth are completely covered, let it stand for a few hours until it has hardened. When it is good and hard mix a thicker goo of plaster and water and stir in some sawdust or coffee grounds. The addition of the coffee grounds or sawdust serves two purposes. One is purely practical. The sawdust or coffee grounds absorb much of the moisture and thus keeps the entire mixture moist and workable, while without it, the plaster tends to dry so quickly that after a few minutes it can no longer be applied except in thick clumps. The other purpose is to create a rough surface which more closely resembles earth than does the smooth surface resulting from the use of pure plaster.

Paint the Plaster

Once all that plaster mess has completely dried we have a rock-hard basic topography consisting of our mountains, valleys etc., all in pure white. Now comes the job of painting everything with some sort of basic coat. This should be quite thorough, because any of that pure white showing up in one corner or another can't help but be very obvious and distracting. What colors to use depends largely on the type of landscape. If the plan calls for

Fig. 4-8. It takes hundreds of such ribs to form a mountain range.

Fig. 4-9. The ribs represent the vertical profile of the topography.

meadows and wooded areas, some shade of green mixed with a bit of brown might be best. If we are thinking in terms of steep cliffs, such as those red mountains in Arizona and New Mexico, a reddish brown might be called for on the steeper slopes. Personally I like to use several cans of pre-mixed colors of some water-based paint, say, one green, one brown, and one red, and, using the same brush without cleaning it when changing from one color to the other. Do a fairly sloppy paint job in which the various colors run into one another. The thicker the paint is applied, the better the whole thing will look in the end.

Texturize

Once that paint has dried, I take a large can of relatively thick rubber cement and spread it over the painted surfaces, one section at a time. Then, while the rubber cement is still wet, I sprinkle sand, dust, dirt, model grass and such all over it, taking pains to have ample amounts adhere to virtually every portion of the surface. Care should be taken that grass is placed where grass would normally grow, while dirt or sand would tend to collect in crevices, creek beds and so on. The more thoroughly the base paint is covered with all this material, the better the final result is likely to be (Fig. 4-10). I might point out here that most of the commercially purchased model gravel, sand, grass etc. is of much too pure a color to give a realistic effect. The best way to use this material is to mix it with some plain ordinary dirt. But be sure that it is dry dirt. Damp dirt tends to collect in clumps and it won't stick well to the wet rubber cement.

What we should have now is the complete landscape except that it lacks trees, shrubs and other vegetation (except grass), rocks, boulders and any type of manmade structures. Before continuing on with any of those additional refinements, we now should complete any as yet uncompleted portion of the trackwork, because the position of the tracks will tend to influence whatever additional landscaping work is to be done.

TREES, SHRUBS, ETC.

Model trees can be purchased ready to use, or they can be made from scratch. Often a mixture of the two will give the most

Fig. 4-10. The more thoroughly the base paint is covered with all kinds of material, the better the final result is likely to be.

satisfactory results. Making one's own trees can be a laborious undertaking, or it can be quite simple. Many purists among modelers will go about the task by creating the basic armature for each tree (the trunk and the branches) from picture wire, and then covering the whole thing with spray glue or rubber cement (very thin), blowing some type of model foliage across it. This will fairly realistically adhere to the glue-soaked wire contraption. The trunk and whatever portions of the branches are not covered with "leaves" will then have to be given a coat of brown paint.

Personally, I find this method too complicated and time consuming. Instead I like to go out into the yard and pick up tiny dried portions of shrubs and grasses which look more or less like miniature trees minus the foliage. I then spray these twigs with spray glue and quickly dunk them, upside down, into a coffee can filled with loose model foliage. In this way I can create dozens of trees of all shapes and sizes in a matter of minutes and I find that they work out quite satisfactorily (Fig. 4-11).

Bushes are something else. For them I use the commercially available lichen. But lichen must be used with care if it is to end up looking the way it should. Instead of using it in big clumps, a better effect is achieved by tearing it into tiny pieces and, using a mixture of different colors, soaking these pieces in thin rubber cement and sticking them together until the desired shape of the bush is

Fig. 4-11. Trees can easily be made from small dry shrubs found in the yard.

achieved. Since much of the commercially sold lichen is dyed in excessively bright, unrealistic colors, it may be necessary to apply a bit of paint here and there.

As anyone who has ever tended a garden knows only too well, weeds are prone to pop up everywhere, and a minute bit of lichen in all kinds of places (Fig. 4-12) will give the layout that "lived-in" look.

ROCKS

The type of mountain landscape which I happen to like is always distingished by rocks and boulders being strewn all over the place (Fig. 4-13). To artificially manufacture such rocks and boulders is not only difficult and time-consuming, it is also unnecessary. Virtually any driveway or country road can provide all kinds of such little rocks which, when placed on the layout, (Fig. 4-14) add much realism. The nice thing about such natural rocks is that their color is real, making everything else look more real in turn. It goes without saying that rocks should be placed where they can realistically be expected to be found. By placing accumulations of gravel and a few tiny shrubs at the base of such rocks, we add one additional touch of reality.

Always make sure that such rocks are firmly in place. It wouldn't do to have one roll down an incline and into a moving train. Again, the ever-present rubber cement is as good a means of securing rocks as any.

RIVERS AND LAKES

Bodies of water tend to be a bit tricky (Fig. 4-15). I have read of all kinds of ways in which modelers have attempted to make water look realistic, some using glass, and I have heard of at least one case where actual water was used. My own method is actually quite simple and, from my point of view, at least, eminently satisfactory.

For the surface of the water, be it a creek, a river, or a lake, I use the white side of composition board. I paint this with a bluish-greenish mixture of water color, making sure that the color is somewhat streaked and uneven. Once that has dried, I apply a thick coat of rubber cement and let that dry. This gives a certain amount of sheen and reflection, but results in a slightly uneven surface which is reminiscent of the movement of water (Fig. 4-16). After that the only thing left to do is to landscape the water's edge with rocks, gravel, twigs, shrubs and the like. The more debris there is at the banks, the better the effect.

Fig. 4-12. Weeds grow everywhere. Lichen, torn into small pieces, can make a satisfactory substitute.

If what we are modeling is a creek or a river in mountainous country, where the water can be expected to be rushing and thus creating tiny wavelets, we might, while the rubber cement is still wet, sprinkle a tiny quantity of that reflective stuff that is sold as

Fig. 4-13. In mountain country, rocks and boulders are everywhere.

Fig. 4-14. Small natural rocks make good boulders.

Fig. 4-15. If there is a river, the water must somehow be simulated. (Note the two, as yet, missing bridges)

Fig. 4-16. A base of composition board, painted with a mixture of light blue, green and dirt colors, and then covered with a very heavy layer of rubber cement gives a satisfactory impression of water.

snow for Christmas trees. But don't overdo it. Just a tiny speck of light here and there is all that is needed to give the desired effect.

BRIDGES

Where there are rivers, there are bridges. The variety of types of railroad bridges found in different parts of the country seems endless. Some examples are shown in Figs. 4-17 through 4-19. And the different model manufacturers have consistently added to the number of kits and ready-built bridges of all types which are available at most every hobby shop. But, as is only logical, in many cases such readily available bridges don't fit into the space where they are needed. Kits can, of course, be modified and adjusted, but more often than not it is a better idea to build the whole thing from scratch. Just pick a prototype that seems right for the particular location and then, using whatever material you feel comfortable with, become a bridge builder.

Fig. 4-17. Where there are rivers, there are bridges. These are near Harrisburg, Pennsylvania.

While in real life bridges need to be constructed to carry a given amount of weight and to withstand the onslaught of winds, floods and what have you, we don't have to worry about that. As long as we start with some reasonably firm support for the roadbed itself, the rest can be constructed of balsa wood, paper, or whatever flimsy material happens to be on hand. As long as it *looks* sturdy, that's all that counts.

ROADS AND HIGHWAYS

Roads and highways are a problem because, except for narrow country lanes, they simply take up an inordinate amount of room, (Fig. 4-20) and spare room is usually what is in short supply on a model railroad. Still, roads are everywhere and without them the layout would look funny. In most instances I have tried to use only short sections of roads, having them run from, say, the edge of the layout into a tunnel in a mountain or into a hidden valley (Fig. 4-21). Thus the effect of the road is there, without the complication of having it go logically from one particular place to another.

Major highways are even worse because one four-lane highway takes up about as much room as would eight parallel railroad tracks. Still, if a small portion of one can be worked in somewhere and populated with cars and trucks, it makes for a pleasing effect.

Any not-too-smooth drawing board of adequate thickness usually serves well as the surface of a road when it is painted a sort of medium grey and dressed up with gravel, shrubs and the like at the edges (Fig. 4-22). And don't forget the telephone poles. There is hardly a road anywhere without telephone lines running alongside. Some fairly decent looking telephone poles (plastic) can be purchased at hobby shops, and telephone lines can then be strung from one pole to the next, using silk thread (light grey would seem to be best). A quick touch of white or aluminum paint on the insulators will make those plastic poles look a bit better. Of course, there is no reason why anyone with enough time and patience couldn't make those poles from scratch. But always remember, it takes a lot of telephone poles to dress up a few feet of road.

Fig. 4-18. A bridge over a dry arroyo.

Fig. 4-19. The bridge over the Rio Grande Gorge near Taos, New Mexico.

Fig. 4-20. Highways tend to take up inordinate amounts of room on a layout.

Fig. 4-21. Here the highway disappears in a double tunnel.

58

Fig. 4-22. Not-too-smooth drawing board makes a good road surface. (Notice that the car appears to be minus its left rear wheel. This is the sort of thing we can easily miss with the naked eye, only to then notice it on a photograph).

And then there are road signs and billboards and what have you. These, too, are available commercially, though billboards are often more fun when we make them ourselves. Practically any magazine has illustrations in its many advertisements which can be used as a billboard. All it takes is a bit of imagination. And highway identification signs, such as US-66 or I-25, can be found in the correct color scheme on some of the road maps which gas stations used to give away free (Fig. 4-23).

CARS AND TRUCKS

Depending on the scale of your layout, there is a variety of commercially available car and truck models on the market. Some, in the larger scales, are quite beautifully detailed, while in the smaller scales, such as N-gauge, they are largely cheap little plastic things which don't look like much. Still, by taking a fine brush and painting bumpers and window frames with aluminum paint and afterwards dirtying them sufficiently to get rid of that plastic look, they can be made to look pretty realistic.

If that doesn't satisfy the more demanding perfectionist, car and truck shapes can relatively easily be carved out of solid balsa wood and then painted. To get a fairly realistic window effect, the window areas should be painted a neutral dark color, possibly with the suggestion of a person, and then covered with tiny pieces of the kind of non-reflecting plastic sheets which are sold in artists/supply stores as non-reflecting picture glass. These should do glued with the non reflecting side on the *inside*, as we do want the car and truck windows to reflect some light.

If the scene we're trying to create is a dawn, dusk or night scene, we might want the car and truck headlights to be lit. Since at least in N-gauge there is no room to insert actual light bulbs, the best solution is to use fiber optics—thin lucite strands which we feed from below the layout through the surface of the road into the bottom of the car or truck, with the ends sticking out of the headlights just far enough to stay firmly in place. Then, by lighting the under-the-layout ends of this lucite strand, the headlights will appear to be lit. It may be necessary to paint these strands black in the area where they go from the road surface into the underneath part of the car or truck, as otherwise some stray light might leak out there.

BUILDINGS AND STRUCTURES

The variety of commercially available buildings and structures in all gauges is quite considerable. They can either be used as they are (Fig. 4-24), in which case the certain amount of dirtying of the outer walls is usually a good idea. One good way of achieving a realistic aging effect is to mix a little bit of grey water color with enough water to permit it to run down the walls of the building (Fig. 4-25) from top to bottom, thus creating the effect that would have resulted from years of exposure to rain.

Not infrequently we may find that the kit structures are not exactly what we want, or that they don't fit into the available space. In that case we may decide to simply use sections of them and combine these sections with scratch-built additions (Figs. 4-26, 4-27 and 4-28). By doing that we can often produce two or more buildings or structures from one kit, each different and unique.

Or we can, of course, build everything from scratch, using balsa wood, the many different shapes of available wood strips, cardboard, paper and scrap (Figs. 4-29 and 4-30). But even then it

Fig. 4-23. The road sign was made by using white typewriter ribbon on black. The I-25 sign (bottom right) was cut out of a road map.

Fig. 4-24. A kit-built structure, somewhat aged.

is usually advisable to include ready-made windows, doors and such, which can be bought in kits or which may have been left over from complete kits previously built. Always be sure to remember to include such details as television antennas, telephone and electric power lines running into the building from a nearby pole, possibly a bunch of garbage pails at one corner, and so on. It's all of these minor additions which make the difference between something that looks like a model, and something else that eventually looks like the real thing. If such a building has a row of windows, have some of them partially open, others closed, possibly include a slightly askew Venetian blind, or curtains drawn to different positions in the various windows.

Skyscrapers (Fig. 4-31) are not usually a good idea on a model-railroad layout. They may be tempting subjects if a portion of a city is included, but their very size is such that they tend to dwarf everything else around them. Still, if it strikes one's fancy, one might want to place a high-rise Hyatt Regency Hotel somewhere near a terminal, adding a certain amount of extra interest by having a lighted outside elevator move up and down the side of the building. If such a building is placed behind some other structures, it might be a good idea to scale it down somewhat. Thus, by being in a slightly smaller scale than what's in front of it, it will artificially add to the feeling of depth.

Fig. 4-25. A lumberyard building, built from a kit.

PEOPLE AND ANIMALS

People and animals are a necessary nuisance. They are necessary because any scene without some sign of life must

Fig. 4-26. A combination of kit and scratch building.

Fig. 4-27. Pieces from several kits were combined in this structure.

necessarily look lifeless and phony. They are a nuisance because the selection of commercially available models is rather limited, and making them from scratch, especially in the smaller scales, is too difficult a task for all but the most ingenious modelers. The smallest size of scratchbuilt figures I know of was in HO-gauge. In this gauge the late John Allen made large numbers of people and animals by constructing an armature of picture wire, then dipping it into wet candlewax, and then carving the individual figures out of the wax. Then an undercoat of white shoe polish was applied, after which the figures could be painted. But I doubt that even he could have done this successfully in N-gauge.

This means that most of us are stuck with what can be bought at the hobby shop, and the best thing to do is to get a lot of such figures and to use them in groups here and there. If too many of them end up looking alike, one can always change the color of the clothing with some paint and a fine brush.

Fig. 4-28. What started as a kit was changed to fit the dimensional needs of the layout.

Fig. 4-29. A clapboard house, built from scrap.

LIGHTS

Most buildings will look better if the windows are lit. The simplest way to achieve this is to have all models of buildings open at the bottom. We then simply run the necessary wiring through the bottom of the layout and attach a light bulb over which the building is then placed. This has the advantage that if the bulb burns out it can be replaced without involving a major dismantling job.

Since in real life the lights we see in the windows of buildings are not all of the same intensity, we might want to cover the windows on the inside with different thicknesses of layers of wax paper, thus causing some windows to appear brighter than others.

The lights used for this kind of illumination should preferably be handled by transformers other than those used to run the railroad. By using cheap little bell transformers and bulbs of the appropriate voltage, it is easy to install whatever added resistors are needed in order to keep the lights from being unrealistically bright.

And then there are signal lights. Signals, again, can be either bought ready made, or they can be scratch built (Fig. 4-32). Either way, they should be wired in such a way that they switch from green to red or yellow and vice versa, depending on the movement of the trains and the position of switches (Fig. 4-33). Many articles have appeared in the different model railroad magazines explaining various ways of achieving this. Since this book deals primarily with photography and not the techniques involved in wiring a layout, suffice it to say that signals are an important ingredient of realism.

Fig. 4-30. A small three-story house, also built from scrap.

Fig. 4-31. Skyscrapers are usually not a good idea on a model-railroad layout.

And for the purposes of photography, they only have to be lit—they don't actually have to work.

THE MOVIE-SET SYNDROME

If a layout or a portion of a layout is built primarily to be photographed, or if it is placed in such a way that observers can only see it from one or a limited number of angles, we can frequently take a leaf out of the book of the movie makers and build structures and scenery only partially. If a house can only be seen from the front, then there is no point in spending a lot of time and effort in detailing the back (Fig. 4-34). Granted, the back may have to be closed in order to avoid spillage of light, but any opaque piece of cardboard will do just fine. The same is true of mountains and other types of scenery—just build what can be seen and don't bother with hidden corners and crevices. As a matter of fact, leaving the back of scenery open, more often than not, is helpful in re-railing or retrieving a car or a train that happened to get stuck somewhere on hidden track underneath the scenery.

EXTRANEOUS ANIMATED FEATURES

Most model-railroad layouts concern themselves primarily with the railroad itself and with scenic features which are directly related to it. But there are any number of other features which may have nothing directly to do with the railroad, but which may be fun to consider.

Fig. 4-32. A scratch-built signal, serving two tracks.

69

Tramways, such as the one near Palm Springs, California, which goes from the desert floor to the top of Mount San Jacinto, or the one near Albuquerque which goes to the top of Sandia Peak, could be modeled and made to actually work.

A heliport could be established on the roof of a terminal or other building, and, using a tiny hidden motor, the rotor blades of an idling helicopter could be made to turn. Or we might include a portion of an airport, partially hidden by mountains in order to avoid having to deal with its huge size. Some airplanes may be

Fig. 4-33. A signal tower, scratch built, at the entrance to a freight yard.

Fig. 4-34. If a structure can only be seen from the front, there is no point in detailing the back.

parked here and the windsock would show the direction of the wind.

The possibilities are virtually endless, limited only by our imagination and the time available to turn them into realistic models.

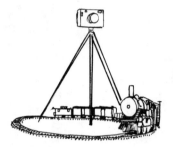

Chapter 5
Choosing Scenes
To Photograph

Most of us, when we first start to take pictures of our model railroad, tend to simply place a train into a given position, somewhere in relation to a piece of scenery we happen to be particularly proud of, and let it go at that. It is only much later, after these simple arrangements are more or less exhausted, that we may consider creating complicated scenes especially for the purpose of coming up with entirely different and unusual photographs. Real life is full of scenes and activity which can be reproduced in miniature (Figs. 5-1 and 5-2) and incorporated into the model-railroad layout.

In this chapter I am listing only a few suggestions which, I hope will serve as thought starters for the more venturesome modelers. Some of these ideas require a considerable amount of extra work and the modeling of special items, while others can easily be accomplished with material which is likely to be on hand.

ROAD CONSTRUCTION

If there is a section of a road or highway on your layout, consider making some signs and barriers which announce that there is roadwork ahead, that the driver must be prepared to stop, and that either all or at least one lane of the road is closed to traffic. Then model some road repair vehicles and equipment, cover the closed portion of the road with dirt and small rocks, and place a bunch of people around. They don't actually have to be digging or

Fig. 5-1. An oil-storage facility.

Fig. 5-2. A busy rail yard.

working. Most road repair crews seem to consist of a whole bunch of people who just stand around while the lone operator of some complicated piece of oversized equipment appears to be doing all the work.

A flagman might be a nice idea. It's easy to take one of the standard model figures and give him a red flag to hold. Then we might pile up a whole string of bumper-to-bumper cars which are waiting to be given permission to continue on along that one available lane or detour.

A scene like this could represent an interesting foreground for a train that happens to be passing farther back. After all, to many of us who enjoy the activity of modeling scenery and scenes, the railroad itself is just sort of a combining factor, one which makes the whole thing hang together. Otherwise we could just model individual scenes in the form of dioramas and forget about the railroad altogether.

Alternately, expecially if you happen to lean toward the morbid, the road might be partially closed because of a traffic accident. In that case there would be the two (or more) cars or trucks which were involved in the collision, plus maybe two or three police cars and an ambulance, not to mention other cars and bystanders.

Here you would have an opportunity to use fiberoptics to create the blue and red lights on the police cars and on the ambulance. And remember to put skid marks on the pavement where one or the other car tried to stop or swerve. A scene like this might best be placed at a blind curve, where the road goes around a mountain or some such.

EARTH-MOVING EQUIPMENT

Some of the equipment used at construction sites and in the process of building new roads or highways, is utterly fascinating in all its intricate detail, not to mention the fact that all that equipment appears to be painted either yellow or orange, making it stand out in its surroundings. The local Caterpillar or John Deere dealer may have illustrated catalogues which can be used to produce a detailed model. If not, any modeler would most certainly be welcome to take pictures of the equipment, or to spend some time there, making detailed drawings.

Any number of scenes can be visualized in which such equipment would play an important role. It may be in the process of cutting away a piece of a mountain in order to make room for a future highway, or it may simply be leveling the ground somewhere. If you happen to be driving past such a construction site in which this type of equipment is being used, stop the car and get out your camera. Take a whole bunch of pictures from different angles, so that you have something to go by later on when you are faced with the problem of incorporating the scene into your layout. Memory is fine, but there is nothing like a real picture to make things look the way they should.

JUNK YARDS

Junk yards, while smelly and not particularly attractive in real life, can add a touch of realism to the layout. Simply pick a place that seems logical for a dump site, and scoop up all kinds of left-over junk and dump it there. Junk yards are full of old boxes, mattresses, broken furniture and bent barrels. Remember that there has to be a road leading to it, usually a narrow dirt road. And it might be a good idea to have a dump truck at the edge in the process of dumping its load.

Or you may like the idea of an automobile junk yard, one of those places which more often then not seem to be located near the railroad tracks, where old automobiles are being stripped of usable parts, or simply sit there rusting and rotting. Just collect all the model cars from all over the layout and place them, more or less helter skelter, onto an appropriate site. Then sprinkle some loose dirt or dust over the whole thing, and you've got it made.

But again, remember that there must be an access road. And there is usually a high wire fence around such places, keeping thieves out and a large dog inside.

A MOVIE COMPANY AT WORK

In the old days relatively little motion picture work was done on location. All that has changed and today the movie people can be found just about anywhere, making motion pictures for either theatre or television. The typical location movie scene consists of a few actors—two or three at the most, a bunch of reflectors, several auxiliary lights on heavy metal stands, a generator to produce current for those lights and for the camera and sound equipment, a camera on a tripod, dolly or even a crane, a sound truck and a microphone which dangles from a long aluminum boom in front of the actors, just high enough to be out of the picture being taken by the motion picture camera. Then there are anywhere from 20 to 50 or more technicians who stand around and watch the scene being shot. There are usually heavy black cables on the ground leading from the generator to the lights and the camera and the sound truck. And then there are all manner of auxiliary vehicles including a mobile kitchen. And on the periphery of the scene being shot are a half dozen or so so-called director's chairs for the director, the script girl, the leading actors (when not in front of the camera) and other more or less important people. Most of these chairs would have either the name of the person who is supposed to use them stenciled on the back, or, in some cases, it will simply say **DIRECTOR, PRODUCER, SCRIPT, or STAR.**

Remember that, just as with the railroads themselves, motion picture equipment has changed over the years. If the layout is based on a certain period other then modern, old-type equipment should be also be used. An exception to this rule would be a case in which an old-style locomotive or train is part of the movie scene being shot. In that case it can be assumed that the movie people are using modern equipment in order to shoot a period picture, possibly a Western.

A DERAILMENT OR RAILROAD ACCIDENT

Derailments are a virtually daily occurrence on model-railroad layouts. In real life they don't happen that often, but when they do happen, the result is usually a great deal more drastic. Cars are telescoped into one another and are strewn about with sections ripped out or bent out of shape. To recreate such a scene in miniature could wreck a lot of good equipment. The best solution would probably be to use as-yet unfinished kit-built equipment and carefully stage the accident scene. Then, when it has been satisfactorily photographed, the unfinished cars can be salvaged and finished as future rolling stock.

Sad to say, magazines like *Time* and *Newsweek* only too frequently have reason to reproduce pictures of train wrecks, and a careful study of such picture can serve as a useful guide.

CHRISTMAS

How about decorating a town or village or whatever populated area we have on our layout for Christmas? Using either fiberoptics or grain-of-wheat bulbs (though they are a bit large), we can hang Christmas lights on the outside of our buildings, and in the town square we might want to erect a large Christmas tree. We might even take color slides of some actual Christmas trees and use them to give the impression of Christmas trees inside our buildings, using the technique described in the chapter on interiors in living color.

This is especially nice if it is done to be ready for the actual Christmas season, when all of us are in a festive mood and attuned to seeing such decorations all over the place. It would even make a nice Christmas card for the following year.

MINING OPERATIONS AND OIL EXPLORATION

Coal and similar mines are a favorite subject for modelers whose layouts include mountainous terrain. The trouble with most available kits is that the result is simply too neat and unused looking. Real mines (Figs. 5-3 and 5-4) are a mess. They are usually crooked jerry-built affairs which started relatively small and then have been added to throughout the years until what results is an incredible jumble of structures. Building one from scratch is a great way to use up all that scrap lumber that's been left over from other projects (Fig. 5-5). The only thing to be kept in mind is that in some more or less logical way the coal must be able to be transported, downhill, from the hole in the mountain to the place where it is then loaded into railroad cars. And remember, everything is

Fig. 5-3. Real mines are a mess.

Fig. 5-4. Another view of the mine. When photographing prototype scenes, always take a lot of pictures from all different angles. They come in handy come modeling time.

covered with black coal dust and incredibly dirty. There is no such thing as a clean looking mine.

An oil-exploration drilling rig is a nice feature. They can be found in some fairly unlikely places in the Rocky Mountains as well as in the plains, so it matters little where they are put. (For years there used to be a producing oil well right in the middle of La Cienega Boulevard in Los Angeles.) Usually, where such a well is being drilled, one will also find those Praying Mantis-like contraptions which indicate a producing well from which the superstructure has been removed.

Operating drilling rigs are kept working day and night and therefore are equipped with a lot of lights, lighting up the entire area. If all manner of extraneous motion on the layout appeals to you, you can install a small motor under the base of the layout to cause the producing-well pump to bop up and down, and if you're a real stickler for detail, you can even motorize the drilling shaft. It would be a nice idea to simulate having brought in a gusher, but, frankly, I can't think of a way of doing that.

SNOW

A snow-covered landscape is not pure white, except possibly at the very top of mountains which remain snow-covered the year

Fig. 5-5. Building a mine from scratch is a great way of using up all kinds of scrap materials.

around. To model a realistic snow landscape, one should first construct the regular landscape with rocks and grass and trees and bushes. Everything should be finished the way it would look without snow, right down to the paint. Then spray the whole thing, a section at a time, with spray glue, and then put some powdered sugar onto a piece of paper and blow it onto the scene from the direction from which the wind is assumed to be blowing. If the first application is not enough, it can be repeated several times until the effect looks just right. (But be sure you have no mice in the house, or they'll come out at night and eat the whole layout!) Remember to include some snow drifts, some of which will automatically develop if you blow hard enough. And if a snowplow has cleared a road or track, snow, not too clean, should be piled high by the side of where it has been cleared.

Finally, when the snowscape is just right, one might spray some more spray glue over the whole thing, just to anchor down any remaining loose "snow." But be sure to keep that spray glue off the track. It's murder to remove, once it has hardened.

Maybe a ski run with skiers and a motorized chairlift would be a nice idea on one side of a mountain, with a log-cabin restaurant at the bottom. Just use your imagination.

Chapter 6
Color Interiors,
Lights,
Smoke and Fire

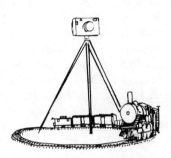

At one time or another it may occur to many of us that it would be nice to see people in the process of doing one thing or another through the open doors or the windows of buildings, or to see passengers through the windows of passenger cars. The obvious way to achieve this would be to scratch-build actual miniature figures in whatever attitudes we are after. While this is certainly possible, it also calls for an incredible amount of work and, in turn, time and patience, so much, in fact, that most of us will soon decide to discard the whole idea.

INTERIORS IN LIVING COLOR

But there is another and very much simpler way to obtain the desired effect. This way involves the use of our camera. What we need to do is to decide what we want to see through those windows and doors and the actual size of the image in relation to the scale in which we are working. Having made those determinations, we now take our camera and take pictures on color transparency (direct positive) film, such as Kodachrome or Ektachrome, of the desired scene, making sure that the size of the image on the resulting color slides is of the correct proportion.

We then cut the finished slides to the appropriate proportions of the doors or windows, leaving them just a trifle larger in order to permit gluing them to the door or window frames on the inside of the building or cars. We then take a thin piece of frosted material, such as frosted plastic or glass (many of the plastic sleeves sold in camera stores for the storage and preservation of color slides have

81

one frosted side) and attach this to the back of the transparency. Then, by placing a light inside the buildings or cars, it will appear that what we are looking at are people occupied with one thing or another inside the building or car. It is usually a good idea to place a piece of pure white paper behind the light to act as a reflector, as this will help to distribute the light evenly over all parts of the transparency. A bit of experimentation will show whether it is necessary to use one light source for each window or door, or whether one such light will provide sufficient illumination for several. It depends largely on the type of lights used and on the size of the buildings. For instance, in a long passenger car with a half dozen or more windows, one light will probably be insufficient. In a case like that it may take three or more individual lights to do the trick.

SOURCES FOR SCENES

The question which immediately comes to mind is, where do we get the scenes to be used and photographed for this purpose? We can use family members or friends, if they are willing to cooperate and to devote the time necessary to achieve the desired result.

But there is an alternative solution which, in many ways, will prove a lot better and certainly easier. In all those millions of magazines which clutter up our newsstands there are thousands upon thousands of photographs of all sorts of people, dressed in all sorts of clothes, doing all sorts of things. It shouldn't require more than a few hours of leafing through some magazines to find pictures which would serve our purpose admirably. It makes no difference what size those pictures are. Big or little, either way they can be used. And we don't have to use all of such a picture. Just a small section showing, say, a woman sweeping the floor or a person seated on a chair in just the right way will do perfectly well.

Once we have selected the right picture, we prop it up, making sure that the paper is good and flat, light it with a daylight-type lamp or simply with daylight coming in through a window, and, putting our camera onto a tripod, experiment with the distance between camera and subject until we can be reasona bly certain that the resulting photograph of the printed picture wi.. be of the desired size. We then photograph it, preferably using several different exposures to make sure that the resulting transparency is of just the right density, and then we use the finished slide in the way described above.

Don't pay any attention to the fact that most such publications include a printed warning, stating that reproducing any of the contents is illegal. Granted, it is illegal to do so for commercial purposes or profit, but since what we are doing here is strictly for our own enjoyment and involves no profit motive, there is no reason to worry about that.

In addition to the fact that using existing photographs is a lot simpler than working with live models, it also permits modelers who like to deal in antique trains and scenes to search for pictures in which the people are appropriately dressed in costumes of the period. Finding such pictures may involve a bit more research, and you may find that you have to use realistically executed artwork rather than photography, but in the small size in which it will eventually be used, that should make little difference.

All this may appear to be a lot of effort to achieve something that might be likened to gilding the lily, but for those who delight in a great deal of extra detail, it will certainly prove worth the trouble.

LIGHTING CAR INTERIORS

Once upon a time when model-railroad car trucks were still made of metal, it was possible to have the wheels of one truck pick up positive electric current while the wheels in the other picked up negative current. This current would then enter the trucks themselves and could be picked up on the inside of the car and used to activate tiny lights. The drawback, even then, was that the lights would be lit only while the train was in motion. Once it stopped because current was cut off from the rails, the lights would go out.

Today, especially in the smaller scales, most car trucks are made of molded plastic, thus eliminating this means of transferring power to the inside of the car. Therefore, if we do want to light up the inside of passenger cars or cabooses, some other method has to be employed. It is, of course, possible to install wipers on the axles and thus still use the current from the rails. But this not only perpetuates the problem of lights being lit only when the train is in motion, it also is relatively complicated and fairly unsatisfactory because dust tends to accumulate, causing interruptions in the flow of the current.

A much better way would seem to be to ignore the current in the rails altogether, and to use a separate and completely independent power source for this purpose. Type AAA penlite batteries are light and small enough to fit even into N-gauge passenger cars and cabooses. The logical answer, therefore, is to remove the bottom of the to-be-lit car and to attach such a penlight battery with a drop of cement. Then run a wire from one end of that battery to a 1.5-volt bulb. The other end of the battery is attached to a second wire which leads to the smallest available on-off slide-switch. We now cut a small hole into the bottom of the car, just large enough the let the moving knob of the slide switch stick out far enough so that either by hand or with the help of a tweezer, it can be moved from off to on and back again. We now cement that switch into that opening and run a wire from the other end of the switch to the other contact on the lightbulb. Then we put the car back together again and, at any time we feel like it, regardless of whether the train is moving or not, we can turn on the light inside it.

Make sure that in positioning the lightbulb inside the car it is not directly opposite a window. The effect is always better if the bulb itself is hidden and all we see is the glow.

If the light from the bulb seems too bright to be realistic, we might want to use two such bulbs in series, or, if that is not practical, we might experiment with a couple of different small resistors (any old radio that has outlived its usefulness can be vandalized for such parts) until we find one that cuts the amount of light to the desired degree.

Don't keep those lights on indefinitely. These tiny batteries do not have a very long life, and replacing them is practically as much trouble as was the original installation. Therefore, the sensible thing to do is to use them only when we are trying to impress visitors, or, of course, when we want to take a photograph which is intended to represent a dawn, dusk or night scene.

And while on the subject of impressing visitors, there is something quite fascinating about operating the layout with all the lights in the room turned off (or dimmed down to a very minimum) and watching the trains with their own lights move through the barely discernible scenery.

CREATING SMOKE EFFECT

Smoke is part of most any realistic scene, but it is also a pain in the neck for modelers. Quite aside from the physical difficulty of producing realistic smoke effects, it is not particularly desirable to end up with a room full of smoke after an hour or two of operating the railroad. Good ventilation, while eliminating that problem, also tends to blow the smoke away so fast that its visual effect is minimized to a point of being meaningless. Thus, except for the few remaining modelers who continue to operate live steam equipment, it would seem to be the better part of valor to forget about smoke altogether in the context of the day-to-day operation of the railroad.

But for pictures it's a different story. When we want to take an exciting picture of a steam locomotive or of a factory or other building equipped with a chimney, to have smoke come from it would seem like a nice addition. The question, then, is, how?

Basically there are two ways to create the effect of smoke. One is to model smoke out of some type of material that can be formed and made to look like smoke under the appropriate light conditions, and the other is to actually burn something that will produce real smoke.

Artificial "Smoke"

The best material to create artificial "smoke" is either cotton or spun glass, and a combination of the two. (Careful: Spun glass tends to break off into microscopic pieces which have an unpleasant habit of sticking into the skin, and itching like mad. It is best worked by wearing rubber gloves.) To produce the desired shape for the "smoke," we first make an armature out of very thin wire. We then paint this wire white to avoid having it show through as some kind of dark skeleton later on. When the paint is dry we immerse the whole thing in a dish filled with thin rubber cement. We then add the cotton/spun glass mixture, a bit at a time to the armature until the desired shape has been achieved. All this can best be done away from the actual layout. When it is satisfactory in shape, and when the rubber cement has more or less set, we can take the finished smoke to the chimney from which it is to emanate and attach it with any available model cement. Since there is no way to make such artificial smoke look completely realistic, it will require a bit of experimentation with the light, side light, back light, whatever, to make it appear as real as possible in the final photograph.

The advantage of this method is that once the smoke has been modeled it can be used time and again, whenever the need arises. In the meantime it can be stored away and nothing will happen to it if it is treated with adequate care.

Real Smoke

Real smoke is a different story. For steam engines in HO and larger scales, smoke pellets can be purchased in hobby shops, but in the smaller scales there simply is no room for them. Since we are talking here about using smoke for a photograph rather than in the context of actual operation, we can set up the picture we want to take in advance and then, when everything is the way we want it, worry about creating the smoke effect as the very last bit of preparation.

In most such instances it will prove virtually impossible to create smoke on top of the layout. It will have to be generated below the layout and somehow directed to the places where it is needed, be it the smoke stack of a steam engine or the chimney of a factory or building. This, then, involves a smoke source and a system of plumbing to get it to where we want it.

The smoke source can be anything, a smoke or incense pellet, a slightly damp rag in a non-flammable container, or simply a cigarette or cigar. If the smoke source is such a pellet or rag, the entire system has to be designed in a way which is similar to a fireplace. In other words, there has to be a means of an air intake near the bottom where the actual burning is taking place. Then there has to be a funnel-shaped smokebox to collect the rising smoke. The top of this funnel is then connected to some sort of thin and preferably flexible tubing which is fed through holes in the base of the layout to positions where the smoke is supposed to appear. In the case of buildings and such it can simply be run up into the chimney. With reference to steam locomotives it is more complicated. Since it is unlikely that it is possible to actually feed the tubing through the inside of the engine into the chimney iteself, we may have to fake it.

We can run it up the far side (the side away from the camera) of the engine and attach it with a drop of cement to the far side of the chimney. Then, if the picture is taken from an angle which more or less resembles the eye-height of a human being standing level with the track, the smoke will appear to be coming from the chimney. Since there is often a certain amount of steam coming from beneath such an engine too, we might want to take a pin and punch a hole into the tubing level with the wheels to cause some of the smoke to escape there. This may require that the tubing be bent just above the pin-prick, as smoke always takes the easiest way out, and there must be some resistence to its progress in order for some of it to use that extra hole.

It will probably be necessary to blow some air into the firebox in order to create a sufficient amount of smoke and also, in order to keep the burning material from going out. The kind of rubber-ball-equipped gimmick that is used for basting a turkey is good for this purpose. An actual fireplace bellows may also work, though it might be too powerful and cumbersome. As with just about everything else, a certain amount of experimentation will be necessary before the desired effect can be achieved.

If a cigarette or cigar is to be used as the smoke source, it eliminates the need for the fire box and the smoke box. All that is needed is the plumbing, such as described earlier, but extended far enough from under the layout to be reached by either the person who is taking the picture or by a helper. Smoke from the cigarette or cigar is then blown hard into the tubing, forcing it to escape at the proper moment in the proper places.

Once this whole system has been made to work, we are still faced with the question of how to light it for the best effect. There is no hard and fast answer for this. It depends primarily on the color of the background. If the background is very light, we may want to keep most of the direct light off the smoke to have it appear dark against the light background. If the background is dark, we may want to side-light or back-light the smoke in order to make it stand out light against the darker background. The best thing to do is to place lights consecutively into different positions and then create some smoke and see what it looks like. Then, when we've finally come close to the type of image we've been envisioning all along, it's time to actually take the picture.

By the way, electrical supply houses sell something that is known as "spaghetti." It is plastic insulation, usually black, without any wire inside. It comes in a variety of sizes, and can be used for the plumbing. Its primary advantage, aside from low price, is its total flexibility. An alternate means might be those flexible drinking straws that can be bought in grocery stores. The trouble with them is that they are short, and it will require attaching quite a few of them to one another in order to achieve tubing of the appropriate length.

Smoke is not something to get involved with too often, but it's kind of fun to play with when plenty of time is available.

FIRE

Building a realistic appearing model fire for still photography is virtually impossible. For motion picture photography it can be done. The primary reason is that fire has no constant shape. In order to get a reasonably realistic effect we need the constant flicker, and that requires motion.

The best method I have found is an adaptation of those phony fires we see occasionally in store-window displays where fireplace tools are sold. In such displays we often find a fireplace which produces a flickering orange light which, when we don't look too closely, does give the impression that there is a fire in the fireplace. The effect is created by the use of an orange gelatin sheet, a banged-up tin can with shiny surface, and an electric light bulb hidden either below or behind the tin can. The tin can is attached to an electric motor which turns it continuously at something like five or six revolutions per second. The light from the light bulb is unevenly reflected by the banged-up shiny side of the tin can, lighting up the somewhat crumpled sheet of orange gelatin at uneven intervals.

A similar arrangement, probably quite a bit smaller, can be constructed underneath the base of the layout, completely screened from the outside so that none of it can be seen. Then, through an opening in the base of the layout the flickering light can be directed into the inside of a house in which we want to pretend that there is a burning fireplace, or to any other place where we want the impression of a fire.

As long as we've gone to all that trouble to construct such an artificial fire, we might want to consider modeling a burning building complete with fire trucks, fire hoses and all the other paraphernalia associated with fighting a fire. In such a case, if we want to give the impression of flames shooting out of the roof or upper windows of the building, we can attach thin strips of that orange gelatin to the opening in the roof or the inside of the windows. We then place a small electric fan under the layout in a position which will cause the air stream from the fan to be blown into the inside of the "burning" building. This will cause those gelatin strips to blow upward and outward and being illuminated by the flickering light of the "fire" they will give the impression of leaping flames.

But don't forget, it's the motion that creates the illusion. A still picture of such a scene is likely to look like nothing at all.

Chapter 7
Using The
Real World

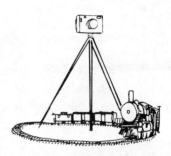

What about taking our models outside and photographing them against real backgrounds—real mountains, trees, buildings, stations, freight yards? With patience, time, and a certain amount of experimentation, some interesting effects can be achieved (Fig. 7-1). First and above all it means scouting around for just the right location which will provide the setting we are looking for. Once that has been found, we'll have to experiment with where to put the model in relation to the selected background.

Obviously, nothing that is real such as a tree, a bush, or even a blade of grass, can be anywhere near the model, as the size difference would instantly ruin the impression we are after. Any item in the immediate vicinity of the model must be to scale. Everything real will have to be quite a distance behind the model where its size will automatically be reduced by perspective (Fig. 7-2).

SELECT THE PROPER LENS

Once the physical relationship between the model and the real-life background has been established to our satisfaction, we'll have to start looking through the camera to see which lens, if any, will give us the effect we are looking for. The problem we'll be running into here is that it is unlikely that any lens other than a very short focus wide-angle lens, even when stopped down all the way, will give us the depth of field necessary to keep both the model and the background in sharp focus. But, using a wide-angle lens will increase the effect of distance between the model and the background, an effect that will only partially be offset by the fact that everything in that background is actually much larger than it should be relative to the model.

Using longer focal length lenses will force us to keep the camera a considerable distance from the model. This would mean that the picture we are after will occupy only a fraction of the negative or color slide, requiring a considerable degree of subsequent enlargement to give us what we are after.

USING A PINHOLE CAMERA

The ideal method to produce the necessary depth of field and a perspective which will make the model look as if it actually belonged into the scene is the so-called pinhole camera. The principle of a pinhole camera is simple: Light entering a lightproof box through an extremely tiny hole will produce an image on the rear wall of that box, and if that is where the film is, it will expose the film, resulting in a photograph. No lens of any kind is needed.

In practice, any standard camera can be converted into a pinhole camera by removing the lens and replacing it with some sort of lightproof cylinder, closed in front except for the pinhole. Depending on the distance of that pinhole from the lens, the image being seen by the film will be comparable to that resulting from the use of lenses with varying focal lengths.

The advantage of this method is that the depth of field is, for all practical purposes, infinite. The disadvantage is that the amount of light exposing the film is so minute that we may find that we have to resort to very long time exposures. With the camera on a firm tripod, this should present no major problem, assuming that nothing in the background moves during that exposure. If wind causes tree branches to move, or if someone suddenly starts to walk around somewhere in the background, then we're in trouble. Also, we have no way of knowing what the right exposure might be. It's strictly a matter of trail and error. Anyone wanting to try this might consider the following procedure:

Use An Exposure Meter

Get everything set up and use an exposure meter to get a clear idea of the amount of available light. Let's say that the exposure meter tells us that with the film we are using we would need a 1/50 of a second at f/16. This then gives us a basis on which to gauge

Fig. 7-1. What about taking our model outside and photographing it against a real background?

future exposures. We now expose our picture with the pinhole contraption for 30 seconds, one minute, two minutes, four minutes and so on. Depending on the film being used and the amount of available light, it may take less exposure or a great deal more. The best idea is to use a roll of black and white film and shoot a whole roll with different exposures, making notes as to which frame was exposed how long. We then develop that film and find out which frame represents the best exposure.

Check the Results

Let's say that the best exposure is four minutes. That means that in relation to what the exposure meter told us, the actual exposure needs to be 200 times as long. Knowing that, we can use that information in the future at any time at which we want to take such a picture. For instance, let's assume that we used Plus-X film for the test exposures. Plus-X has an ASA rating of 125. Now, the next time we want to use Ektachrome-400 which has an ASA rating of 400, we can use the exposure meter with the same setting as before. This time it will tell us a different exposure, say, 1/25 of a second at f/16. We now multiply 1/25 by 200 which results in eight minutes. But the film is 3.2 times as fast, so we now divide eight minutes by 3.2 which gives us 2.5 minutes or two minutes and 30 seconds. Or we can adjust the exposure meter to read in terms of ASA 400, and it will read the exposure as 1/80 of a second (25 times 3.2 equals 80) and we now multiply that by 200 to arrive at the same 2.5 minutes. In other words, we have established a frame of reference by which to use the exposure meter (either the one built into the camera, or a separate one) to determine the right exposure for our pinhole camera.

But this is reliable only as long as the distance of the pinhole from the film remains unchanged. If the distance is either increased or decreased, a new test roll will have to be exposed to arrive at a new figure by which to multiply the exposure meter reading. (Increasing the distance of the pinhole from the film will increase the required exposure, and decreasing the distance will reduce the amount of exposure needed).

Ideally, the construction of one of those pinhole attachments should consist of a short cylinder, one end of which must be designed to fit into the lens fitting of the camera itself, making sure that there is no light leak. Then a second cylinder, a bit larger in diameter, should be fitted over the first one with either the inside of this second one or the outside of the first one lined with black

Fig. 7-2. Real backgrounds have to be a considerable distance from the model in order to appear to be in scale.

velvet to assure that no light leaks through. The second cylinder is the one that is closed in front with just the pinhole opening in the exact center. Now the second cylinder can be moved back and forth, thus changing the focal length of the "lens," and, in turn, changing the amount of the scene which is projected onto the film (See Fig 7-3).

All of this is a lot of work and only the individual modeler can decide whether it is worth the trouble.

THE RAILROAD IS JUST AN EXCUSE

There are a considerable number of hobbyists among model railroaders who, if they want to be honest, don't really care much about the railroad itself. They love modeling scenery, buildings, and all that sort of thing, and the railroad is simply there as a means of having it all hang together. Those among use who feel that way should possibly ask themselves if using the railroad in such a manner is worth the effort and expense. After all, there is no reason on earth why they couldn't simply spend their time building models of whatever turns them on, and, once having eliminated the railroad altogether, there is no longer any constraint with reference to scale. Granted, one has to work to some kind of scale to make things look right, but this can now be any scale that happens to be practical.

Building an entire small town or village, either modern or of some period in history that seems interesting, could be a task that would keep us out of mischief for months if not years.

Petroleum refineries are incredibly intricate and might represent a worthwhile challenge, as would offshore drilling platforms.

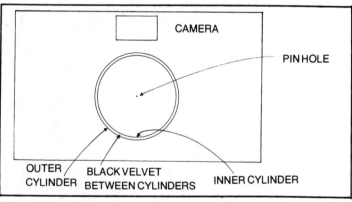

Fig. 7-3. Any standard camera can be converted to a pinhole camera.

Fig. 7-4. Here is an intricate freeway interchange; this one in Cincinnati, Ohio, which might be fun to model.

Or how about one of those intricate constructions where several freeways join and pass over and under each other (Fig. 7-4). The famous Los Angeles interchange where the Hollywood, San Bernardino, Harbor and Pasadena Freeways meet is a good example. In building a project like that it would be a good idea to find out in advance to what scale a good selection of miniature cars and trucks is available at an affordable price, and then to work to that scale.

Even just a section of a big city, say New York's Times Square or the Grand Central Station section of Park Avenue could be a lot of fun, with all those skyscrapers. By installing individual banks of illumination for the buildings and the streets, and operating them through some type of switch panel, one could produce the different lighting effects for dawn, day, dusk or night. Or, how about a busy harbor?

And, in the context of what we are concerned with in this book, any of these suggestions as well as hundreds of other ideas could be the subjects for interesting photographic studies. As with the railroad, don't necessarily think in terms of photographing the whole model. Get in close and pick interesting sections and angles, always remembering that the camera should be in a position which would be logical for a scale-person.

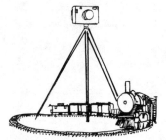

Chapter 8
The Effect Of Motion

As a general rule railroad trains are thought of as something in motion, and occasionally we may want to create the effect of motion when we want to photograph a stationary scene with a train moving through in the background. There are two basic ways in which this effect can be achieved, both of which call for a certain amount of preparation and considerable precision, possibly coupled with a bit of luck.

ONE METHOD OF PHOTOGRAPHING MOTION

The first method calls for a particular scene in the foreground which we want to keep in sharp focus while a train is moving through behind the scene at a right angle to the camera. Here we set up the camera on a tripod (Fig. 8-1) in front of the scene to be photographed and we focus on the scene itself, stopping the diaphragm down far enough to obtain the depth of field needed to also hold the background in reasonably sharp focus. We now light the scene with the amount of light needed to permit us to use a time exposure of somewhere between a half and one second. We now place the train on the track just beyond the edge of the picture and determine what rheostat setting will be needed to cause it to move across the entire picture in the time of the exposure. Then, while the film is being exposed, we run the train through the background.

What we'll get here is a sharp foreground scene and a sharp background with the train appearing as a blur. If we want to see the train somewhat more clearly, we might place the engine in such a

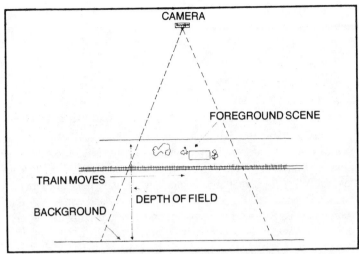

Fig. 8-1. The camera is held steady on a tripod during the time exposure while the train is moving through the scene.

position that its front end is stationary in the picture as we start the exposure. Then, while the film is being exposed, we advance the rheostat to the appropriate setting and have it move through. Alternately, we can have the train move into the picture while the film is being exposed, and then stop it somewhere in the picture before the end of the exposure.

This kind of thing takes a lot of experimenting, and you may find that you'll have to shoot it a dozen times or more before achieving the desired result. A good suggestion might be to try it first in black and white since black and white film is a lot cheaper. Then, when you have found which method produces the right kind of an effect, you can repeat the procedure in color.

ANOTHER METHOD

A different way of producing the effect of motion calls for the rain to remain in fairly sharp focus, while the foreground and background are blurred. In other words, what we are striving for here is the image which might result when we follow the moving rain with our eyes, focusing on it rather than the fore and background.

In this case we have two moving objects to deal with and this will require even more experimentation. What we are trying to do to have the train move through the scene at a given speed and, gain using an exposure of, say, one half to one second, to pan the camera at a speed identical to that of the movement of the train. In this case it is extremely important that both the track and the camera itself are perfectly level, as otherwise the horizontal position of the train in the picture will move either up or down, resulting in an undesirable vertical blur.

Width of Scene Important

Using this method calls for a number of prerequisites which do not apply to the method described earlier. One has to do with the size of the subject-scene being photographed. Since the camera must be panned (Fig. 8-2) during the exposure, it will "see" a great deal more of the layout than it does when it is held stationary. Thus, the width of the scene (not the height) and especially the width of the background must extend three or more times to either side than would be necessary otherwise. Even though the foreground and the background will be blurred, it wouldn't do to have some unrelated image intrude at either end of the exposure.

Most likely you will find that having the train move at a very slow speed, thus permitting the camera to be panned quite slowly, is easier to accomplish with a necessary degree of precision, and, in addition, it will require less scenery to be included in the picture. Also remember that with the train moving at right angles to the camera position there will be a change of its distance from the lens, and if this change is too great, it may exceed the available depth of field.

Consider Using a Second Person

Furthermore you might find that this is really a two-person operation. There are a number of more or less simultaneous actions involved here which are difficult for one person to perform. One: The train must be started. Two: The camera lens must be opened and must be made to remain open for the length of the exposure. Three: The camera must be panned by hand in a manner which will keep the train continuously in the same position in the picture. Four: The camera lens must then be closed.

Since it may prove cumbersome, if not impossible, to keep depressing the cable release while, at the same time, panning the camera, a better idea might be to use one of those cable releases which has a hold-screw which when tightened, will keep the lens open. In that case we can hang a cover over the lens then open it with the cable release and secure it in the open position. Then, when we're ready to start the exposure, we simply remove the lens

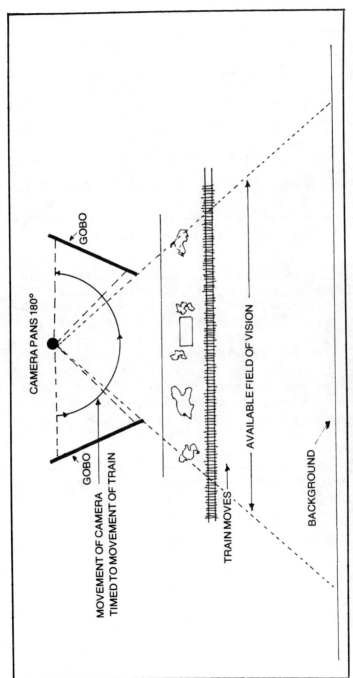

Fig. 8-2. As the train moves through the scene, the camera pans with it.

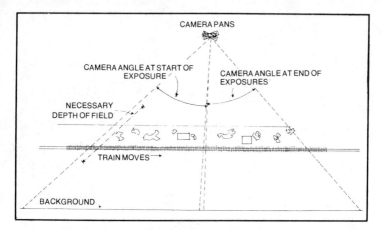

Fig. 8-3. Place a gobo just beyond the right and left end of the scene being photographed.

cover, perform the panning action and then replace the lens cover, after which we can release the set screw to close the lens.

There is another way to do this. Place a black (preferably black velvet) gobo just beyond the right and left end of the scene being photographed (Fig. 8-3). Be sure everything in the room, except the actual scene being photographed, is in total darkness. You can now point the camera toward one of the black gobos and open the lens. With no light reflecting off the black velvet, no exposure will result. You then start the train and as it appears from behind the gobo you pan the camera with it until it disappears behind the other gobo. You can then close the camera lens at leisure.

All this may seem like much to-do about very little, but with practice and a bit of luck some really fascinating results can be achieved.

Chapter 9
Using Photos to
Create Scenery

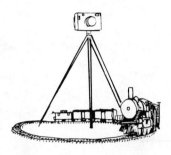

So far we have talked primarily about ways and means of obtaining effective photographs of the model railroad and the scenery on the layout. In this chapter we'll examine some of the techniques which can be employed in using photography in the process of actually creating certain scenic details which are hard to scratchbuild realistically, especially in the smaller scales. What it amounts to, in brief, is to take a picture of the prototype to be modeled, and then to use that actual picture, or rather portions thereof, on the layout.

Let's think for a moment of all those different signs which are found along the right of way as well as on every road and highway. Along the right of way all of these signs are in black and white, while most highway signs use color. So we'll take the black and white signs first.

ROAD AND HIGHWAY SIGNS

It is difficult and, for most of us, actually impossible to model these signs in their correct scale and hand-paint the appropriate lettering, especially if we are working in N- or even HO-gauge. On the other hand, the available selection of such signs which can be purchased in stores is limited, and the majority of those which are available has that cheap stamped-out-of-plastic look. Granted, they can be aged and bent to look crooked and worse for wear, as many of the prototypes do, but even then we are limited to the few legends which the manufacturers offer.

Photograph Actual Signs

Now here is a way to make our own signs; actually two ways. The first, and by far the best, is to go out with the camera loaded with black-and-white film to the nearest location where such actual right-of-way signs can be found. We now take a bunch of pictures of those actual signs, not at an angle but straight on, preferably not only the sign but also the post or stand to which it is attached. Be sure that there are no shadows across the sign from a nearby structure or tree. What we're looking for is a flatly lit, plain, ordinary, straight-on photograph of the sign. It makes no difference what size it is within the dimensions of the negative. It also makes no difference what there is in the background, as we'll eventually eliminate the background altogether.

Make Prints

We now develop the film and make a print. Here we have several options. If the image on the negative is smaller than the actual model of the sign is supposed to be, then we can make an enlargement to just the right size. If, by coincidence, it happens to be just the right size, we can simply make a contact print. If it is larger than the dimensions of the scale sign, we'll need to reduce the image. But since few photographers or camera shops are equipped to handle reductions, (photostat people do make reductions, but usually at a considerable loss in detail) it is a better idea to make a sharp enlargement which can subsequently be rephotographed to the correct size.

Cut Out the Photo

The object of all this is to eventually cut out the sign, if necessary attach some stiffening to its back, employ the usual means of aging it with a bit of dust or dirt, and then place it on the layout. Ideally, for this purpose, that final print should be made on smooth matte or semi-matte double-weight paper. Glossy prints cause too much reflection, and single-weight paper doesn't have enough body to hold its shape.

Rephotograph the Enlargement

If you feel that your dexterity may not be quite up to doing a neat job of cutting out something as small as that, there is an alternative method which makes it a bit simpler. Instead of making a print of the desired size, we make an enlargement to, say, 5×7" or 8×10", this time on glossy paper, single weight. Now, having a large image, it is easy to do a good job of cutting out the sign itself. Then, with rubber cement, we glue the cutout onto a stiff black cardboard. This pasteup we then rephotograph to obtain a new negative showing only the sign on a pure black background. We now make a print of the desired size on matte (or semi-matte) double-weight paper. Now we still have to cut that out, but with everything around the subject being pitch black, the cutting doesn't need to be quite as precise, because minor irregularities will not show up. Be sure to paint the edges of the paper in dull black, as the paper itself is, of course, white.

Using Transfers

Now, assuming that the type of sign you're after is not conveniently available anywhere that you know of, or that for one reason or another it is impractical for you to go out and take a picture of an actual prototype; there are two alternatives. One involves leafing through all available model railroad and actual railroad magazines for a picture of the desired sign. If you find one, you can photograph the reproduction in the magazine and use it as if it were the prototype picture you would have taken yourself, if that had been possible.

Make It Yourself

If you can't find what you're looking for, the only remaining solution is to make the sign yourself. But, as we said earlier, making it to scale is a near impossibility. So, what we'll do instead is to make it in a much larger size. In this case, let's, for the time being, forget about the stand and concentrate on the sign itself. We'll draw the outline of the sign, assuming it has a black border as most of them do, with India ink to the correct proportions. Now comes the job of lettering. Few of us would be able to do a decent hand-lettering job, even in such a much larger size. So, unless you're an expert hand-letterer, don't try it. All artists supply stores carry something called *transfer letters*. These are transparent wax-coated sheets of some type of plastic on which there are letters, numbers, and all manner of other frequently used designs and signs. The available variety is quite enormous, and I can think of little, if anything, that you might need that is not available in this form. (These stores have books which show all available styles and types, and all the different sizes in which they come.) You now use these transfer letters (they are simply rubbed onto the paper) to produce whatever lettering the sign requires. If you find that you have difficulty keeping these letters straight, draw a line with a non-photo-blue pencil and use it as a guide. The blue will not show when photographed with black-and-white film.

Now, having hand-made the sign or signs (one can actually make dozens in a very short time), we photograph our handiwork and follow the same steps described earlier. Again, if cutting out tiny images precisely is a problem, paint everything around the hand-made sign black (or cut it out and paste it on a black cardboard) before photographing it.

Unless you have your own darkroom in which to make your own prints and enlargements, you might now wonder how to tell the camera shop to give you prints of your negative of exactly the right size. Telling them that you want the final image to be one and an eighth inch high may not do, as these people usually make all kinds of prints for amateurs, and are attuned only to worry about the outside dimensions of the final print. It is much safer to simply tell them that you want your full negative printed without cropping, and that the print should be of a given proportion. There is a simple method to arrive at this proportion, and this is illustrated and described in Fig. 9-1.

Colored Signs

So far we have talked about black-and-white signs. But what about color? As a general rule colored signs are highway or road signs and are therefore more easily accessible to use than are the

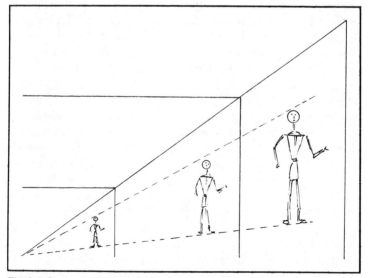

Fig. 9-1. By drawing a diagonal line through a picture from corner to corner we can find the correct overall size of the desired enlargement (reduction) to get the subject to the size we need.

signs along the railroad right of way. We can, therefore, eliminate the problem of painting such signs ourselves on our drawing board. Instead we either take a Polaroid-type camera, or our regular camera loaded with color-*negative* film and go out and take pictures of all the signs we want to use on the layout. We then have prints made of those negatives or we use the Polaroid positive prints, cut them out, paste them on black cardboard as described before, and rephotograph them again. Here, too, we can use either Polaroid-type film, in which case it is important to take the picture from exactly the right distance to get the correct size of image for the scale in which we are working, or we can use color-negative film and then have a print made to the correct proportions (but be sure that the negative image is either of the actual size to be eventually used, or smaller, as obtaining a reduction will be difficult).

When rephotographing a color print, be sure to use either daylight or artificial light which is the color of daylight, as ordinary artificial light will cast a yellow glow over the whole thing, unless the film used is designed to be used with such artificial light.

BILLBOARDS AND AD SIGNS

This method of using photography is by no means limited to road- or right-of-way signs. It can just as easily be used to produce billboards, all manner of advertising signs, you name it; anything two-dimensional that we see in real life can be photographed, printed to the correct proportions and transposed to our layout.

There are even ways to transpose such photographic images to the uneven outside walls of buildings. Since most photographic paper is too stiff to be formed to follow the indentations and protrusions of, say, a brick or clapboard wall, we can carefully peel off most of the paper from the back of the photograph until, what we have left is a very thin sheet consisting of the (undamaged) emulsion and just a slight layer of paper. We now cover the wall of the building or surface to which we want to attach the picture with a coating of water-soluble adhesive (colorless!) and we soak our picture in water until it is wet through and through. Then, with the building or surface lying on its side, we place the picture on top of it, press it down carefully with a damp cloth until it has taken on the surface roughness of the base, and then let it lie in that position until it has thoroughly dried. Then, by doing a bit of aging here and there, we have a realistic representation of an advertising sign or whatever that was painted directly onto the side of the building, wall, or other surface.

BUILDINGS

There is also a way in which photography can be used in order to simplify the task of scratch-building model buildings. The obvious, of course, would be to take a picture of the structure to be modeled, and then simply use it as a guide. But how about this? You take a straight-on picture of each side of the building to be modeled. But be sure it's straight on to eliminate, or at least minimize, any distortion. This can be done in black and white. Color would be of no value here. You now make prints of the image in the exact size in which it is to appear on the layout. What you've got now are photographic images, to scale, of all the walls of the to-be-constructed building.

The next step is to cut it out, leaving some tabs at the edges which can be bent back. You then glue the whole thing together and what you've got is a photographic template of your model. You may want to strengthen it on the inside with strips of wood or heavy cardboard to make it sturdy and easier to work with, because this is by no means the end of it. This represents simply the base on which to build the actual model. Using the photographic image as a guide, we now overlay it with whatever material we want to use to construct the walls, recesses, window sills, cornices and so on, shaping everything to fit the underlying image. It's fun and relatively easy to do, and the result, if carefully executed, is likely to be more lifelike than if we had tried to do the same thing without using the photographs as a base.

The more you think about how to use photography in your modeling work, the more ideas are likely to come to mind.

Chapter 10
Photos For Record

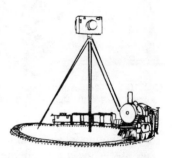

Throughout most of this book I have concentrated on the various techniques involved in producing dramatic life-like photographs of model railroad scenes. But every so often we are less concerned with such dramatic images than with simply producing a photographic record of a piece of equipment, a scenic detail, the looks of a layout in the process of being built, or the layout as a whole.

REMOVE ITEM FOR LAYOUT

When it comes to creating a photographic record of a piece of rolling stock or an individual scenic detail, it is usually a better idea to remove the item to be photographed from the layout and to place it into neutral surroundings with a plain white, grey or black background (Fig. 10-1) in order to eliminate all possible distracting elements. What we are after here is to show every bit of detail as clearly and sharply as possible which, depending on the size of the object, will usually mean getting very close to the subject, involving the use of close-up lenses. We will then probably find that we will have to use the smallest available f-stop in order to achieve maximum depth of field.

Rolling Stock

In the accompanying photographs (Figs. 10-2 through 10-24) I have taken a number of pieces of rolling stock and several scenic items and placed them on a white base with a neutral background.

Fig. 10-1. To obtain photographs strictly for the record, it is better to remove the subject to be photographed from the layout and place it against a plain background.

These photographs are simply a record of items which I currently have stored away because the layout for which they were built has since been dismantled. They can be used to act as a guide in modeling duplicates or similar structures or equipment, or they can simply serve as a reminder of what is already available the next time I decide to start building a new layout.

Commercial Kits

The rolling stock shown here (Figs. 10-25 and 10-26) is commercially available, and has simply been dirtied up and in some instances modified, in order to make it look more realistic. The scenic structures are built from commercial kits.

Fig. 10-2. A Pennsylvania Railroad passenger diesel engine.

Fig. 10-3. A Santa Fe freight diesel.

LAYOUTS UNDER CONSTRUCTION

When it comes to creating a record of a layout under construction, we have a great deal more leeway in the angles, composition and lighting used. Here we don't really care much about drama or beauty. What we are after is showing the method of construction, and so on; showing what is beneath the surface and what will never again be seen, once the layout is completed and landscaped. With all the armature in place, cheesecloth is then stretched across it and soaked with wet plaster. Once the first coat of plaster has dried, additional coats are added. For these coats I like to mix the wet plaster with sand or coffee grounds to achieve a

Fig. 10-4. A 2-8-8-2 articulated steam locomotive.

Fig. 10-5. A 0-8-0 steam engine.

Fig. 10-6. Pullman cars.

Fig. 10-7. Observation car.

Fig. 10-8. A sugar freight car model.

surface roughness which, after it is painted, is more realistic than the smooth surface which would otherwise result. See the chapter on landscaping for greater detail with reference to construction details and tricks.

WIDE ANGLE LENS USEFUL

To get an overall picture of the layout may not be possible, depending on the size of the layout and the height of the ceiling of the room in which it is located. We will probably have to use the

Fig. 10-9. A gasoline freight car.

Fig. 10-10. A miscellaneous flat bed freight car.

Fig. 10-11. Tank freight cars.

Fig. 10-12. More freight cars.

Fig. 10-13. A detailed look at a Western Pacific freight car.

Fig. 10-14. A leased freight car.

Fig. 10-15. Another type of freight car.

Fig. 10-16. A low freight car.

Fig. 10-17. A loaded Erie Lackawanna freight car.

widest-angle lens available, but even then we'll most probably have to shoot portions of the layout (Fig. 10-27) from different angles in order to end up with a reasonably meaningful record of the track-design, landscaping, etc. Such pictures are rarely of interest to anyone except the modeler himself, because, to the uninitiated, they are simply too messy. Still, they tend to serve the purpose of acting as a reminder in future years of what we built at one time and then, subsequently, dismantled.

In this type of photograph (Fig. 10-28) it doesn't usually matter if edges of the layout, walls of the room, bookshelves, windows and the like are included. Later on, if such extraneous matter seems to bother us, we can simply cut away the unneeded portions and paste the remaining section onto a white or black sheet of paper. The best method for cutting out a portion of a photograph, especially if it includes uneven lines, is to take a sharp knife, such as the corner of a razor blade, and cut just the emulsion of the print along the edge of the image. Then, by pulling the paper toward the bottom and toward the part of the picture to be saved, we'll end up with a very thin edge which, when subsequently pasted onto a new base, will not leave any highlights or shadows along the cutting edge.

In the context of keeping a record of past layouts, there might be more that we want to keep track of than just the layout itself.

Fig. 10-18. A good year freight car.

Fig. 10-19. Details of a Santa Fe freight car.

Fig. 10-20. More detailed work.

116

Fig. 10-21. A caboose.

Fig. 10-22. End-on shot of a caboose.

Fig. 10-23. A European-type freight car.

Fig. 10-24. Another European-type freight car.

Fig. 10-25. A kit-built factory building.

Fig. 10-26. A kit-built lumber-yard building.

One such may be the control board as is shown in the acompanying photograph (Fig. 10-29), or some of the wiring.

BE ALERT FOR REAL SCENES

But quite aside from taking photographs, "just for the record," of our modeling accomplishments, it is often valuable when

Fig. 10-27. We'll usually be able to only photograph portions of a layout at a time.

Fig. 10-28. Here it doesn't much matter if the wall of the room, bookshelves and the like, are included in the picture.

traveling around the country to have a camera handy, just in the event that we run into some scene or structure which might lend itself to reproduction in the scale of our railroad layout. Here are some photographs (Figs. 10-30 through 10-49) which I took over the years, many taken from the air when I was flying around in a little airplane. All of these were taken for the specific purpose of being reminded of some scenes that might be good prototypes for modeling. Figure 10-50 shows a model made from the photograph in Fig. 10-49.

Fig. 10-29. The control board of a long-ago dismantled layout.

Fig. 10-30. Railroad running through an oil-storage yard and past a refinery.

Fig. 10-31. A freight yard at the outskirts of a city.

Fig. 10-32. A large freight yard.

Fig. 10-33. A factory building and shipping facility complex.

Fig. 10-34. Various spurs going off a freight yard. Anyone who is interested in modeling an actual situation like any of these shown here, might consider having a huge blowup made of the photograph, scaled up to a size which would cause the distance between the individual rails in the photograph to coincide with the scale distance to be used. It will provide a clear idea of the amount of space that will be needed.

123

Fig. 10-35. A coal-loading facility.

Fig. 10-36. A hairpin turn of the Atchison, Topeka and Santa Fe Railroad, just east of Santa Fe.

Fig. 10-37. The bridge across the Rio Grande Gorge.

124

Fig. 10-38. A roundhouse, no longer in use. This one is near Las Vegas, New Mexico.

Fig. 10-39. Turntable and roundhouse.

Fig. 10-40. The station at Lamy, New Mexico. This is the prototype which was used for the model in this book and in several of the color photographs.

125

Fig. 10-41. Another angle of the same station.

Fig. 10-42. A train coming into Lamy. Photos like this illustrate the camera position which should be attempted when photographing a model.

Fig. 10-43. A closer shot of the same.

Fig. 10-44. This is the kind of perspective which is particularly hard to achieve when photographing a model.

Fig. 10-45. Obviously, model railroaders are not the only ones who occasionally do a sloppy job of laying track.

Fig. 10-46. A good example of a simple road crossing.

Fig. 10-47. This church is the prototype for the one shown in several color photographs.

Fig. 10-48. An Indian cliff dwelling which served as the prototype for the model shown in the book.

Fig. 10-49. A photograph of the site of the Indian cliff dwelling at Puye Cliffs, which helped in creating realistic surroundings for the model.

128

Fig. 10-50. The model of the Indian cliff dwelling which is based on Fig. 10-49. It is made entirely of kitchen matches.

Chapter 11
Photography As A
Means Of Critique

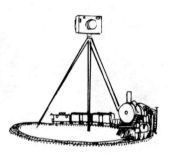

Photography is potentially relentless. Just as in an unretouched portrait it will clearly show every wrinkle and blemish in the subject's face, so will a "portrait" of your model rolling stock or structures reveal all manner of minute flaws which may be virtually undetectable with the naked eye.

My guess is that most modelers are perfectly satisfied if the product of their efforts looks just fine on the layout. After all, how many viewers would take the trouble (and be so impolite) to examine everything through a magnifying glass.

THE CAMERA MAGNIFIES

But that, of course, is what, to all practical terms, happens when a camera is pointed at the subject. Once an enlargement is made from the negative, or once the color slide is being projected onto a big screen, there are those flaws, all nakedly exposed for everyone to see (Fig. 11-1). What this means is that whatever we model with an eye toward eventually photographing it, will have to be executed with more care than would otherwise be necessary. In order to make sure that we haven't overlooked anything, it may actually be a good idea to take a black and white picture of what we eventually want to immortalize in color, and to blow that picture up to 8×10" or 11×14". We can then examine that blowup at leisure and correct whatever we find to be an obvious flaw. If necessary, this can be repeated several times until whatever will be seen in

Fig. 11-1. The enlargement shows that the wall at the second story of the model is poorly installed, something which all along had escaped the naked eye.

the final picture is in a condition of perfection which we find satisfactory.

Then, of course, there are those among us, who take pride in being absolute perfectionists. To them every item on the layout, every component, structure or piece of rolling stock must be able to withstand close inspection under a magnifying glass or even microscope. To them photography can be an invaluable tool. Any model, or even any small section of a model, can be photographed in extreme close up. Then a blowup can be made to be used to study the workmanship, and corrections and improvements are then undertaken on the basis of what the photograph shows.

POTENTIAL TROUBLES UNCOVERED

Similarly, if we put a camera onto the track and take a picture along a more or less straight section of the right-of-way, we'll suddenly see where there are minor kinks or irregularities which are unnoticeable with the naked eye, but which may be the harbingers of future operational trouble.

As a matter of fact, the more we get used to using our photographic equipment in conjunction with our modeling efforts, the more we are likely to begin to wonder how we ever managed to get along without it.

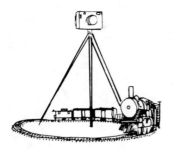

Chapter 12
Color Photography

It's always exciting to photograph your layout in color. This chapter describes different scenes in several layouts which I've photographed in color. You can refer to the color section located on pages 145 to 160 to see the shots described here.

HI-BALLING AROUND THE CURVE

These are two deceivingly simple photographs of an N-gauge freight train, supposedly in the process of barreling around a curve. They are taken from the exact same position, but the effect of the two is entirely different. In Color Plate 1 we have the locomotive, the telephone pole and a good portion of the rails in sharp focus, and the freight cars, though out of focus, can be clearly distinguished in the background. What can also be seen is that I failed to install telephone lines on the telephone pole. It isn't a bad picture, except that it does not seem to give the impression that the train is actually in motion.

In Color Plate 2 everything is, in fact, the same, except that by using a wide-open f-stop the depth of field has been reduced to less than an inch. The only portion which has remained in sharp focus is the very front of the locomotive, with everything else becoming fuzzy and blurred. The result is the impression of the train coming toward the photographer out of the fog, moving at considerable speed.

Lighting

The lighting is, in fact, actual daylight from a partially covered window in the rear wall, with the white walls in the rest of the room providing enough reflection to give whatever illumination was needed to accentuate the detail on the shadow side.

Lens

The lens used for both these photographs was the 50-mm lens with three Vivitar close-up lenses. In Color Plate 1 the diaphragm was stopped down all the way to f.16, resulting in the considerable depth of field, despite the fact that the camera was only about six or so inches from the subject. In Color Plate 2 the diaphragm was kept wide open at f/1.8, with the exposure reduced accordingly. This picture, by the way, even though it shows virtually nothing of the layout, is one of my favorites among all the hundreds I have taken.

THE INTERSTATE HIGHWAY

Most of the time it proves difficult to include a four-lane highway on a railroad layout because such highways take up an inordinate amount of space, and, as a general rule, space is at a premium. On this particular layout I did include a short section of such a highway, leading from the edge of the layout (Color Plate 3) uphill along a short S-curve (Color Plate 4) into twin tunnels (Color Plate 5). The cars and trucks are commercially available models made to look more realistic by the addition of dirt, luggage on the roof and so on. As always, the trick in getting some good pictures of this section of the layout was to find a camera position which could reasonably be expected to represent a place in which a human observer could be found (other than an airplane). As appears obvious in these paragraphs, the countryside is quite mountainous. It can thus be assumed that the cameraman stood atop a hill, overlooking the highway scene.

Lighting

All three of these photographs were taken with actual daylight shining in through an off-scene window, and a white cardboard on the opposite side to lighten up the shadows just enough for the necessary detail. The only artificial light used are the two red tail lights in the tunnel, actually two plastic rods inserted into the tunnel from the bottom with a red bulb hidden underneath the layout itself.

Lenses

Three different lenses were used here. Color Plate 13-3 was taken with a 50-mm lens, stopped all the way down for maximum depth of field. Color Plate 4 was achieved by using a 28-mm wide-angle lens to increase the effect of depth. This one, too, was stopped all the way down to keep the focus as sharp as possible from the extreme foreground all the way to the background. For Color Plate 13-5 I ended up using the 100-mm position of my zoom lens which helped to bring everything closer to the camera than it actually was. I usually don't like to use long-focal-length lenses for this type of photography, but there simply was no other way to get the camera sufficiently close to the subject. Here, too, I used the smallest available f-stop in order to obtain maximum depth of field. In each case the exposures ran to several seconds because the film used had a sensitivity rating of 64 and the available light was considerably less than it appears to have been when one looks at the resulting photographs.

AVOIDING SHADOWS

Here we have a picture (Color Plate 6) of a bend in the river with a train passing in the background. It could have been good, but it didn't really turn out well for the very simple reason that I ended up with a shadow on the background. Apparently I didn't notice that when I took the picture, as otherwise I'd certainly have tried to change the key light to an angle which would have minimized if not eliminated it.

Because of the cramped quarters in which we frequently have to work when photographing small portions of the layout, avoiding shadows on the background can prove to be difficult indeed. But, one way or the other, it has to be done, because it totally ruins the effect of realism since the viewer knows immediately that what he is looking at is a piece of cardboard or a wall, not the sky.

If I remember correctly I was primarily concerned with making that river look realistic, with getting the right kind of reflections off the "water" and the "pebbles" which was probably the reason that I missed that dumb shadow.

LAMY STATION

Color Plates 7, 8, and 9 are of a not-too-realistic representation of the Lamy station, the station at which travelers disembark when they take the Atchison, Topeka and Santa Fe Railroad to Santa Fe. (The Santa Fe Railroad never made it to Santa Fe because of its location in the foothills of the Sangre de Cristo

Mountains. Eventually a pretty rugged freight spur was built to the city proper, but all passengers have to leave the train at Lamy, some 18 miles south of Santa Fe.)

All three are photographed from approximately the same distance from the subject, but at different angles and with different light. Probably the most realistic one of the three is Color Plate 7 which was photographed from the lowest camera angle, with some bushes in the foreground which seems to indicate that the photographer is standing at the side of the road, this side of the gully. The picture was taken during the middle of the day with actual daylight provided by an off-scene window. Despite its being obviously daytime, the lights in the station are on, adding a touch of depth and color. The realism of the scene is spoiled somewhat by the fact that the road past the station seems to abruptly stop at the tracks, which doesn't make a great deal of sense. The station, by the way, is built from scratch out of ordinary cardboard. The car, truck and locomotive are ready-made products, as are the crossing gates (which I had always wanted to automate, but never did).

The second picture in the series, Color Plate 8, was taken from pretty much the same angle, but some time later, after the road was extended across the tracks to the parking lot. This time the light was provided by a standard 100-watt electric light bulb which was covered with a light blue gelatin filter to minimize the amount of yellow in that type of light. Still, the difference in the color of the light, and the fact that the overall lighting is much more flat than in the first photo, has changed the appearance of the picture considerably.

The third of the group, Color Plate 9, was shot at night when there was no daylight available through the windows from the outside. The angle, reminiscent of an aerial photograph, is considerably less realistic, because there seems to be no logical way for a photographer to be up that high. What makes this photograph interesting is the lighting. Again a 100-watt bulb was used, but this time without gelatin filter, retaining all the yellow in the illumination. By placing the light to one side and quite low, we now have the impression of a picture taken at either sunset or sunrise. The resulting high contrast and unrelieved blackness of the shadows, while losing some of the detail, add to the drama of the resulting image.

PUEBLOS AND CLIFF DWELLINGS

Living here in northern New Mexico, surrounded by Indian pueblos and cliff dwellings, it seemed logical to me to want to model some of those unusual structures. One of the important considerations, to my mind, at least, is to stick to subjects with which I am reasonably familiar, because otherwise I feel that I am likely to end up with something that structurally somehow doesn't seem to make sense.

Most of the Indian pueblos are communal dwellings in which each individual room or group of rooms is a part of a larger whole, sort of a forerunner to today's apartment houses and condominium complexes. Several of these are located atop barely accessible mesas, and it seemed logical, therefore, to build one on top of one of the mountains on my layout.

In Color Plates 10, 11 and 12 we have three different views of the pueblo. It consists of a triangular communal dwelling, plus a circular kiva, which is a ceremonial chamber, virtually always round, which can be found in every such pueblo complex. Also typical are the outdoor ladders, as none of these dwellings have indoor stairs. The model you see here, in order to simulate the adobe construction, was modeled out of bread dough (four water, and salt), cooked in the oven and then left to harden. Once hard, it was painted the typical adobe color, plug a few touches of blue around the window frames. As I understand it, the reason the Indians always use blue for their window frames is that it is supposed to repel unfriendly spirits.

The three photographs described above are of a section of a layout which was subsequently dismantled. But I saved the pueblo itself, and incorporated it into a part of a subsequent layout, (Color Plate 13). Here I got a little more ambitious. I placed the pueblo itself into the far background, then added a church in the style of the Spanish churches which were built in all the pueblos during the several centuries during which the southwestern United States were, in fact, a part of the Spanish kingdom. As a prototype for this church I used the Cristo Rey church here in Santa Fe.

Then, since the whole thing sat atop a steep cliff, I decided to build a cliff dwelling, based on those found in the Puye Cliffs on the Santa Clara Pueblo reservation. To create that brick effect I built the whole cliff-dwelling out of kitchen matches, cut into tiny pieces and glued together. Again there are the inevitable outdoor ladders which can be found wherever Indians live or lived.

You will notice that there is no sign of the railroad anywhere. On this layout the tracks ran past that section way down below the cliffs (plus a return-loop section hidden underneath the cliffs), and this scene simply served as an interesting background.

THE MOON

The effectiveness of Color Plate 14 is primarily due to a lighting effect which, I must admit, was actually more or less an accident. The camera was placed in a position which might logically resemble a person looking at the scene from an off-scene overpass. The blue background is, in fact, a window in the room with the blue sky beyond it. And here is where the accident came in. A single light was used in a position above and behind the camera for the purpose of lighting up the shadow areas just enough to keep them from going pitch black. This light created a reflection in the window glass, giving the effect of a full moon being up in the sky. I hadn't planned that when I set up the picture, it just happened to work out that way.

The lens used for this pitcure was a 28-mm wide-angle lens, stopped down to f/16, and the exposure time was one full second. Even using that small f-stop did not result in a sufficient depth of field to keep the detail in the foreground in sharp focus, but the resulting amount of fuzziness is, to my mind, at least, acceptable. As is typical of wide-angle lenses, the perspective is exaggerated, giving a feeling of depth to the picture which would not have been possible with a lens with a longer focal length.

THE FREIGHT YARD

In setting up the scenes in Color Plates 15 through 24 I tried to place all the various ingredients, engines, cars, automobiles etc., in such a way that an impression of great activity is created. Nowhere, here, was I concerned with shooting a "portrait" of any one piece of equipment or structure. The whole effort was aimed toward atmosphere.

To me this is the sort of thing that makes photographing the model railroad such an enjoyable and satisfying pastime. But it does take time. One can easily spend hours upon hours moving things around one way or the other, checking the effect in the viewfinder, making sure that the depth of field is sufficient to keep everything, or at least the important portions in sharp focus. And then there is always the question of lighting. Backlight will produce reflections on the rails and will greatly add depth to the picture. But, of course, there has to be sufficient front fill-in light to retain the necessary detail in the shadow areas.

This series of ten photographs, all taken on a very small portion of the layout, is actually an addition to the basic layout which was built in order to accommodate a station. As can be seen in the "aerial" shot (Color Plate 24) the tracks emerge from the basic layout (upper center of the picture), pass by two motels, curve around the turntable and continue on toward the station area which is out of the picture at the bottom and to the left.

The turntable was built from scratch, and most of the structures are combinations of kit parts and scratch building.

And when it comes to composition, don't ever worry about cutting off sections of the subject you are photographing. Tightly cropped pictures in which the action appears to be continuing past the area covered by the actual photograph are a lot more effective, than those in which everything seems to stop right at the edge.

As can be seen only too clearly in some of the prototype photographs included in this book, especially those taken from the air, most railroad areas are messy and filled with all manner of junk. Nothing will make a photograph of a layout or a section of a layout look more unrealistic than scenes in which everything is nice and neat. Clutter it up with whatever is at hand. The more the merrier. And, as always, don't forget to light up some of the windows in buildings. Not necessarily all of them. But a light here and there adds immeasurably to the overall effect. And add a few people here and there. You don't need many, but a few of them do make a whole lot of difference.

THE GRAVEL ROAD

Here we have a corner of a creek, sections of two railroad bridges, and one of those dreadful dirt roads which are the cause of much wheel-alignment trouble in New Mexico (Color Plate 25). Everything except the rolling stock and the automobile is scratch built, and I must admit to grave doubts about the ability of that stationwagon to continue on on that road, but, be that as it may, the scene as a whole again gives the impression of movement and action, largely because of the composition which excludes all extraneous detail.

The picture was taken with a 28-mm wide-angle lens, stopped down to the smallest available f-stop. The camera was on a tripod to permit a time exposure, as the light used was simply the available reflected daylight emanating from various windows in the room.

Looking at the picture closely, I have the feeling that the railroad bridge closest to the camera is less than structurally sound. This is one of those typical instances where sloppy modeling work, which is barely noticeable with the naked eye, shows up only too clearly in a close-up photograph.

THE EDGE OF THE LAYOUT

Here are two different angles of a scene located right at the front edge of the layout, which made positioning the camera easy, while making it difficult to keep the edge of the layout out of the picture. In Color Plates 26 and 27 the fact that the edge of the layout can clearly be seen effectively ruins the impression of realism. What I should have done, but obviously didn't do, was to temporarily construct some type of foreground scenery which would have provided a screen for that portion of the photograph in which the edge of the layout appears. Actually, this could have been done quite simply by placing a few bushes and shrubs near the camera. In addition to screening the edge of the layout, it would have served to give the impression that the camera was located in a place in which an observer could logically be expected to be standing.

In Color Plate 27 another disturbing feature is the edge of the window which can be seen in the background to the far right. That window provided the light for both these pictures, but some kind of a temporary background should have been installed to screen that section of the wall.

LONG SHOTS

This series of pictures (Color Plates 28 through 32) is typical of the kind in which the model looks like a model, with little if any attempt made to achieve realism. In all of them the camera is at a position which could logically only be achieved by flying over the scene in an airplane. Granted, these pictures show all or large portions of the layout and, in those terms, represent a record of one of the layouts which was once built but has since been dismantled. But that's about it.

All of these pictures were taken with a wide-angle lens, stopped all the way down, and most of the light used was daylight coming in from windows located at either end of the layout.

THE LIGHTED HOUSE

Here (Color Plate 33) we have another case where the fact that the layout was built directly against the wall resulted in a nearly unavoidable shadow on the wall. The picture would have been considerably improved if a sky-color background had been inserted between the scene and the wall, and if a separate light source had been used to light up that background sufficiently to kill the shadow. But that light would have had to be shaded in a way to avoid having it spill over onto the scene itself, as that would have flattened out the picture, reducing the feeling of depth.

As it was, the light used was daylight from the windows in the room, plus, of course, the lights inside the house. Why those people who live in that house have all their lights on when it is obviously the middle of the day, I have no idea.

SUNSET

Color Plates 34 through 38 is a series of sunset effects. In each case the film used was daylight film, and the light was provided by a 100-watt bulb. What resulted was the kind of coloring which we can expect from the setting sun, just before it disappears behind the horizon. In several of these pictures the background, consisting of pieces of cardboard stuck behind the layout, intrudes unpleasantly. It would have been better to use a pure black background which would have caused the lighted portions of the scenes to stand out more distinctly. In all of these photographs the light source was kept quite low, to one side or the other. This is important as the warm light emanating from the rising or setting sun would never come from a high angle. All of these photographs were taken with a wide-angle lens, stopped all the way down.

RECONSTRUCTING A MINE

On a trip through southern Colorado some years ago, I came across a coal mine which fascinated me for some reason, and I took a bunch of pictures of it with the idea of eventually modeling it for my layout. As I soon found out, any attempt to reproduce this mine in every detail in N-gauge would not only have involved an inordinate amount of time, it would probably also have been beyond the capability of my occasionally clumsy fingers. Therefore, instead of following the pictures exactly, I attempted to scratch-build a model which would at least give the general impression of the prototype (Color Plates 39 and 40).

What you see in these two photographs is the result of this effort. I built the mine separately on its own base, and subsequently designed a portion of the mountain to accommodate it. The whole structure consists of thin wood strips, glued together without any template, and subsequently painted black which, with all those hard-to-get-at crevices turned out to be a monstrous job. But once I had it installed, it did look rather like that original mine, which gave the impression of having been constructed, a piece at a time, with no clear plan and by people who certainly never thought of themselves as architects.

The trouble was that the place at which I put it on the layout turned out to be relatively inaccessible and no matter how I tried, I never could get a really close picture of it.

THE CANYON

Here we have a canyon (Color Plate 41) in the mountains with some natural rocks in the foreground and the canyon walls, modeled out of plaster, in the background. The greenery is a combination of trees and bushes made from shrubs found outdoors, plus some lichen and model grease.

The lighting is daylight from various windows in the room, some shaded to keep the light from going too flat. The lens was again the 28-mm wide-angle lens stopped all the way down. I don't remember the exposure, but my guess is that it was something like a half a second.

DEPTH OF FIELD

While most of the time I prefer to keep everything in the picture as sharp as possible, in Color Plate 42 I felt that by keeping only the engine in focus and letting everything else become blurred, I'd end up with a more effective picture. I used the 50-mm lens with the # close-up attachment, and stopped down just enough to produce a depth of field of something like two inches, just enough to keep what we see of the engine in sharp focus.

The light area in the back is actually a window in the room which provided all the light used in this picture.

Not everyone looking at this picture will agree, but to me the fact that everything short of the locomotive is out of focus seems to give the impression of movement. A picture like this is largely a matter of personal taste.

THE MOTEL

The railroad is quite incidental in Color Plate 43. What we have is a small motel stuck away near a country road somewhere in the mountains, with a swimming pool and a parking space in front of it. Judging by the number of cars parked in the parking lot, the motel currently has only three guests, though another one appears to be driving up in a green car.

In the extreme foreground a side road passes across the railroad tracks and a freight train apparently has just passed through, judging by the caboose which is still in the picture. (In fact, when I set up that picture, there was no train at all. I simply placed the caboose where it can be seen, to give the impression that a train had just passed.)

The entire scene was lit primarily by daylight from windows in the room with a white piece of cardboard near the camera position to add a little reflected light. The lens used was a 50-mm lens, stopped down to the smallest available f-stop, and the exposure was a half a second.

OUT OF THE FOG

This is another one of those photographs (Color Plate 44) in which the lack of depth of field is the primary reason for its effectiveness. By using a 50-mm lens with all three close-up attachments, and by leaving the lens wide open, the depth of field was reduced to something on the order of maybe an inch or so. The sharp-focus area was concentrated on the front of the engine, with everything else allowed to go way out of focus.

The picture was shot against backlight, daylight from a window in the background which, being completely out of focus, is unrecognizable. Also behind the position of the engine there were some model lights, signals or some such, I frankly don't remember. These lights created those octagonal shapes which add to the overall impression that the engine is coming at us out of the fog.

HEIGHT PROBLEMS

All these miscellaneous scenes, (Color Plates 45 through 48) suffer from the common fault of having been photographed from much too high a camera position. They were originally photographed on two different layouts.

Color Plate 1. Most of this photo is in sharp focus.

Color Plate 2. See the difference when depth of field is reduced.

Color Plate 3. The highway starts at layout's edge...

Color Plate 4. ...continues along a short S-curve...

Color Plate 5. . ...and disappears in twin tunnels.

Color Plate 6. Wall shadow spoils photo.

Color Plate 7. The most realistic shot.

Color Plate 8. Note the change lighting makes.

Color Plate 9. More interest from lighting.

Color Plate 10. One view of the pueblo.

Color Plate 11. Another view.

Color Plate 12. A third view.

Color Plate 13. The pueblo in a subsequent layout.

Color Plate 14. Notice the importance of lighting.

Color Plate 15. Trains moving through.

Color Plate 16. Many trains on the track at once.

Color Plate 17. A busy lumberyard.

Color Plate 18. Another business located by the railroad tracks.

Color Plate 19. The railroad district.

Color Plate 20. A motel along the tracks.

Color Plate 21. More activity.

Color Plate 22. More accommodations.

Color Plate 23. And still more.

Color Plate 24. An aerial view.

Color Plate 25. Details are important.

Color Plate 26. Realism is lost.

Color Plate 27. This would be much better if the layout's edge did not show.

Color Plate 28. An aerial shot of the layout, just for the record.

Color Plate 29. Details of a curve and track layout through a mountain tunnel.

Color Plate 30. A long shot.

Color Plate 31. The couch doesn't matter in this layout photo.

Color Plate 32. Another layout section for the record.

Color Plate 33. Even though it's obviously daytime, the lights are on in the house.

Color Plate 34. The layout as dusk approaches.

Color Plate 35. Daylight still visible just at the tip of the mountains.

Color Plate 36. In this view, the sun has just started to set.

Color Plate 37. A black background would have been more effective here.

Color Plate 38. The sun's setting can be felt in this scene.

Color Plate 39. Several phases of a mining operation.

Color Plate 40. A closer view of the mine.

Color Plate 41. The shrubbery here is a combination of real and model.

Color Plate 42. Blurring gives the impression of motion.

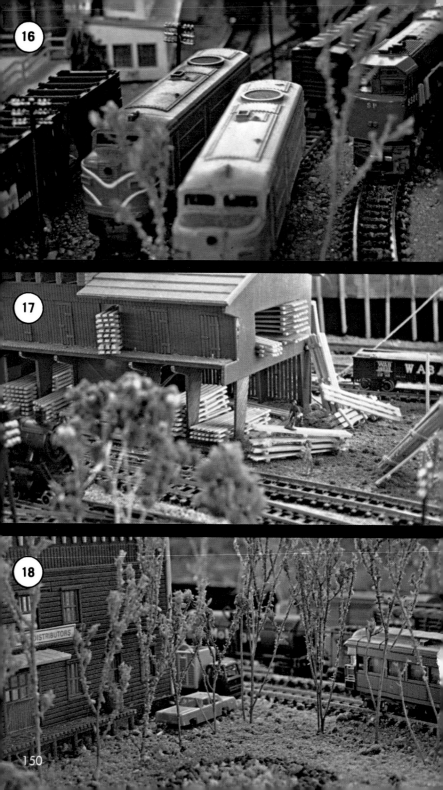

19

20

21

151

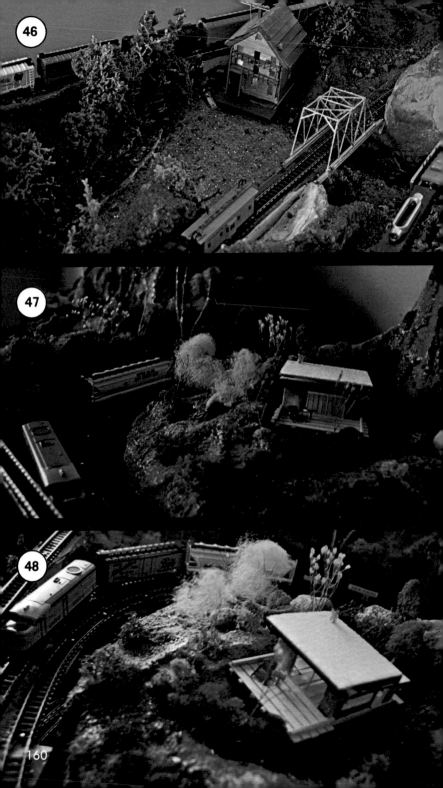

Chapter 13
Let's Make Movies

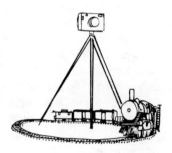

So far all we have talked about is still photography. But there is another facet of photography that must be included if this book is to be complete—motion pictures. With home movie equipment, whether it uses film or video tape having achieved a high degree of popularity, it is only logical that the model railroad enthusiast may want to make some movies of his layout in action. While many of the technical considerations discussed earlier—lenses, lighting, composition—apply to motion pictures as well as they do to still photography, the making of a good, exciting motion picture involves many considerations which are absent in still photography.

LIGHTING IS IMPORTANT

From a purely technical point of view, one of the primary differences to be kept in mind is the amount of light needed to achieve adequate exposure. While in still photography even the minutest amount of light is sufficient because there is no reason why we can't expose the film for several seconds or even minutes, in motion pictures the exposure time is fixed by the number of frames to be exposed and subsequently projected per second (usually either 16 or 24). Furthermore, as in still photography, because we usually will, be quite close to the subject being photographed, very small f-stops have to be used in order to assure an adequate depth of field.

As far as lenses are concerned, a standard lens, a wide angle and a zoom lens will again suffice, though zoom lenses should be used sparingly, as discussed in greater detail later in this chapter.

The greatest difference between still and motion photography is in terms of preplanning. In still photography we simply set up a scene and then photograph it from one or several angles, hoping to produce at least one really outstanding image. Not so with movies. Here motion is the important consideration. Anything that could normally be expected to be moving, but fails to do so in our film, will tend to stand out as a false note. This automatically eliminates the use of model people except, possibly, someone sitting down somewhere, half asleep, and it eliminates automobiles and trucks, unless during the period of time during which we see them on our film they happen to be logically stopped by a crossing gate, stop sign, red traffic light, road construction, accident, or traffic jam.

USE A TRIPOD

Many a home-movie maker may simply decide to put his camera on a tripod (do not, under any condition, attempt to make such motion pictures without a tripod. The unavoidable jiggling effect of hand-held movies is vastly exaggerated when the subject is small and therefore close to the camera), to run his trains and to roll his film, keeping it rolling while the train moves throughout the layout. The result, I'm afraid, can't help but be pretty dull.

Good motion pictures do not consist of one or a few long sustained scenes. On the contrary, they are made up of very large numbers of short scenes which are carefully edited in order to produce the desired effect. But short scenes don't lend themselves to be spliced together to make a logical sequence, unless they are carefully planned in advance.

WRITE A SCRIPT

It may seem excessive to talk in terms of writing a script for such a home movie, but that is exactly what has to be done if the final result is supposed to be worth the effort involved. A decision must be made, in advance, about what the film is supposed to show, and then a shooting script must be prepared, outlining each scene in considerable detail. In order to illustrate what is meant by all this, I have written the opening sequence of an imaginary motion picture (Fig. 13-1) involving the makeup of a freight train and its eventual movement along a section of a layout.

162

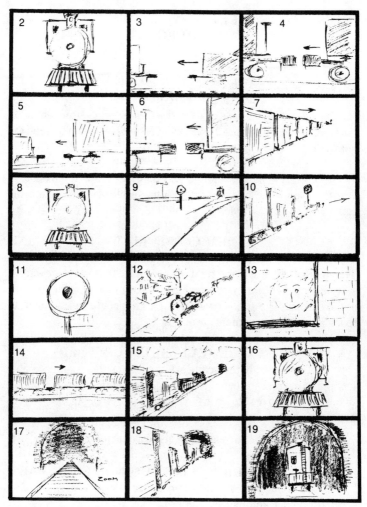

Fig. 13-1. A simple storyboard for the scene described in the text.

SOUND EFFECTS HELPFUL

You will note that in this sample script I have included sound effects. If the movie you may be planning to make is silent, simply ignore the references to sound. On the other hand, if you are equipped to handle sound, these effects are available on sound-effects records, or you can take your tape recorder to the nearest actual railroad yard and record such effects yourself. But don't use the sounds emanating from your model railroad. They are unrealistic and of no value in terms of the finished film.

Scene 1   **FADE IN:**
           TITLES AND CREDITS
           FADE OUT

Scene 2   **FADE IN:**
           CLOSE UP - ENGINE
The camera lens is as close to track level as possible, shooting the front of the engine head on, preferably close enough to keep the smokestack of the engine out of the picture.

SOUND: The hissing of escaping steam and possibly a whistle blast. The engine starts to move slowly away from the camera, going backwards.

Scene 3   **MEDIUM CLOSE SHOT —TENDER AND ONE FREIGHT CAR**
The tender moves from right to left into the scene toward a stationary freight car, part of which is seen standing on the left side of the screen. The action continues until the couplers are about to touch. Keep the movement quite slow.

Scene 4   **EXTREME CLOSE UP - COUPLERS**
All to be seen in the scene are the two couplers and possibly just the extreme ends of the tender and the freight car. The coupler of the tender moves slowly from right to left, engaging the coupler of the freight car.

SOUND: Metal on metal as couplers engage.

Scene 5   **MEDIUM CLOSE SHOT—FREIGHT CARS**
The freight car jerks a bit, then moves slowly from right to left toward a second stationary freight car.

Scene 6   **EXTREME CLOSE UP—COUPLERS**
The other coupler belonging to the now attached freight car enters the scene from the right and engages with the coupler of the stationary freight car.

SOUND: Metal to metal, as couplers engage.

Scene 7   **MEDIUM LONG SHOT—FREIGHT TRAIN**
The train , now consisting of the engine, tender, and a number of freight cars is seen as all cars jerk backwards a bit as the result of coupling, then come to a stop.

SOUND: A whistle blast.

The train now begins to slowly move from left to right across the screen.

SOUND: The clicking of wheels on tracks. This continues throughout the sequence, becoming faster as the the train picks up speed.

Scene 8   **CLOSE UP—ENGINE**

An angle similar to Scene # 2, but this time the engine is moving slowly toward the camera.

Scene 9   **CLOSE UP—TRACK WITH SWITCH AND SIGNAL**

From a low camera angle shooting along the track toward a switch and a signal. The switch moves from one position to the other and at the same time the signal turns from red to green.

Scene 10   **WIDER ANGLE—SAME AS SCENE # 9**

The engine enters the scene past the camera on the left and continues on past the switch and the signal. The scene continues as the freight cars pass by the camera, until we see the caboose moving past the switch and the signal toward the distance.

Scene 11   **CLOSE UP—SIGNAL**

Signal changing from green to red.

Scene 12   **LONG SHOT—TRACK AND TRAIN**

An angle shot of a straight stretch of track with the train, now moving somewhat faster, coming toward the camera. Along the way it passes a house located near the track. Train is moving from right to left.

Scene 13   **CLOSE SHOT—WINDOW OF HOUSE**

This is a close shot of a section of a real window of a real house. Through the closed window we see a young boy or girl with his or her nose pressed to the glass, ostensibly watching the train go by.

Scene 14   **MEDIUM CLOSE SHOT—TRAIN**

The camera is placed at right angles to the track, ostensibly at the position of the house. The train passes through the frame from left to right. This simulates the point of view of the boy or girl.

Scene 15   **LONG SHOT—TRACK AND TRAIN**
The train is moving from left to right away from the camera toward a mountain range and a tunnel in the far distance.

Scene 16   **MEDIUM CLOSE SHOT—TRAIN**
Head-on shot of the train coming toward the camera.

Scene 17   **MEDIUM SHOT—ZOOM—TUNNEL**
With the camera on the track we shoot toward the tunnel and zoom in on the tunnel at a speed which is more or less commensurate with the speed of the moving train.

Scene 18   **CLOSE SHOT—TUNNEL ENTRANCE**
The train is entering the tunnel. We hold the shot until the caboose enters the field of vision.

Scene 19   **CLOSE SHOT—TUNNEL ENTRANCE**
With the camera on the track we shoot straight into the tunnel and watch the caboose disappearing in the dark.

SOUND: Turns hollow, then fades.

The above section of a sample shooting script, consisting of 19 different individual shots, will eventually represent less than one minute of screen time. Having prepared such a script in advance, it becomes obvious right off that the individual scenes do not have to be shot in consecutive order. Any one of these scenes can be shot out of sequence, if doing so reduces the amount of time and effort involved in setting it up.

Let's examine each scene individually:

FADE IN—This implies that we want to fade from black to the scene. If the camera is not equipped with a fade capability, this can also be achieve by putting the lights used in the scene on a dimmer, and by then bring the light up from zero to full.

TITLES AND CREDITS—If it is worth the bother to produce a more or less professionallly conceived motion pictures of the railroad, it is also worth the bother to give it a title and to give yourself the credit for having produced and directed it. As anyone who has ever gone to the movies or watched television knows only too well, titles and credits can take on any one of a million forms. You may want to simply letter a plain piece of cardboard with the appropriate information, using either hand-lettering or transfer letters, and then simply photograph it. Or you can get somewhat more fancy and put the lettering on black cardboard, photograph it, then roll the film back in the camera and expose it a second time with some position of the layout, the train, an engine, or anything else that might appeal to you as a background for the titles.

FADE OUT—This is the reverse of the fade in. If a multiple exposure is used for the titles, make sure that for both exposures the fade in and fade out occurs at the same place on the film. Professional film makers don't bother with so-called opticals (fades, dissolves, etc.) during the actual shooting of the film. They are subsequently produced in the laboratory. But, in order to do that, a print of the original film has to be made, and you may not want to go to that added expense.

CLOSEUP—ENGINE—By starting the sequence with a close up of the engine, we start with a dramatic "bang" which should help to immediately grab the attention of the audience. You could also start with a long shot, a so-called establishing shot, which shows the audience where we are before going to that close up, but that is simply a matter of personal preference. My own feeling is that starting with the close up is more dramatic. The reason for keeping the top of the smokestack out of the picture is that there is no smoke, and this way we won't miss it. Of course, there is no smoke in the later scenes either, but by that time the audience will be caught up sufficiently in the action to not be particularly conscious of it. If the picture is to be a sound film, the sounds of the hissing steam and that of a whistle blast will be a great help in making the shole scene appear real.

MEDIUM CLOSE SHOT—TENDER AND ONE FREIGHT CAR—Here we place the camera at right angles to the track, with the extreme rear end of the tender in the far right of the frame, and the end of one freight car in the far left of the frame. Between them we should see the surrounding freight yard, buildings, other trains, etc. After the camera has started rolling, we move the tender toward the freight car until the couplers couple. Always shoot a little more film than will actually be used in the edited picture. A certain amount of overlap makes editing easier. Also, cuts from one shot to the next should, whenever possible, take place when there is some action going on in the scene, as this will make the film appear to be flowing more smoothly. Thus, by including the action of the couplers actually coupling in this shot as well as in the next one, we can pick just the right frame in editing to cut from this scene to the next.

EXTREME CLOSE-UP—COUPLERS—Here it is important to get in just as close as possible. Cutting from one shot to another which is very similar in size and angle tends to be annoying. The greater the difference between the two shots, the better. Thus, if we have a close-up lens which permits getting a picture of just the couplers and little else, fine. If we can't get in that close, the previous shot (Scene # 3) may have to be a somewhat wider angle than explained in the script, in order to achieve sufficient difference between these two scenes. In this scene we repeat the coupling action already photographed in the previous scene and then keep the camera rolling as whatever we see of the freight car and tender moves on across the scene from right to left, with the tender finally blocking out most if not all of the scene. Doing this will again give us the necessary action for a smooth cut to the next scene.

MEDIUM SHOT—FREIGHT CARS—This is more or less a repeat of Scene #3, except that this time we are dealing with two freight cars.

EXTREME CLOSE-UP—COUPLERS—This, then, is a repeat for Scene #4. These two scenes could be left out, but by repeating the action at least once, we give a clearer picture of the activity involved in making up a freight train. It could also be repeated several times more, but that may get to be a bit tedious. If the film is to have sound, the sounds associated with the coupling must be in exact synchronization. In this particular sample sequence this is the only instance in which sound would have to be carefully synchronized. The timing of all the rest of the sound effects is not that critical, and with a bit of practice it would be possible to run a tape player along with the projector to produce the sound. Thus, if you like the idea of sound, but are not equipped to handle sound on film (the only sure way to achieve precise eliminating the close-ups of the couplers or to replace them with close-ups of wheels moving or some such, anything which will keep the actual coupling action off screen, so that it doesn't matter too much if the coupling sound is not precisely in the right place.

MEDIUM LONG SHOT—FREIGHT TRAIN—This shot as well as all the medium long shots and long shots in this sequence, must be framed carefully to be sure that all we see are portions of the layout and possibly some plain background. I wouldn't do to have the impression we have taken so much care to create spoiled by including a bookcase, window, door or anything else that reminds us that we are not watching an actual railroad operation.

Since the last few shots were taken with the camera at more or less right angles to the tack, this one might best be at something approaching a 45-degree angle, either from the front of the train toward its rear, or from the rear of the train toward the front. Either way, keep the camera rolling until the entire train, or, at least, most of it, is out of the frame. This, again, in order to make subsequent editing simpler.

CLOSE-UP—ENGINE—Here we place the camera on the tracks and have the train move from reasonably far back toward the camera until the front of the engine is virtually on top of the lens. Later on in the editing process, we'll decide how much of this scene we actually want to include. Don't worry if toward the very end the engine goes out of focus. That part will probably be cut out anyway.

CLOSE-UP—TRACK WITH SWITCH AND SIGNAL— This shot should be taken from the approximate eye level of the man in the engine, shooting away from where we assume the train to be toward the direction in which it will be traveling. What we want to see is the movement of the switch points, and the changing of the signal from stop to go. This is a very short intercut to be used between the previous and the next scene, but keep the camera rolling long enough at the beginning and the end to leave yourself some leeway in the editing.

WIDER ANGLE—SAME AS SCENE #9—We now place the camera quite a bit farther back or use a much wider lens, in order to include considerably more of the track. We then let the train enter from the left and continue on through the switch until it has disappeared around a curve or is otherwise out of the frame. Since we'll be showing the change in signal position as the train passes in the next scene, we don't have to bother with that in this one. You may have noticed that I have continually emphasized the screen-direction of the movement of the train. The term *screen-direction* refers to the direction on the screen in which anything is moving. All action should always move in the same direction from one scene to the next. It is extremely disturbing to see a train (or anything else) move from left to right in one scene and then have it move from right to left in the next one. Whenever a change in screen direction becomes necessary for one reason or another, a so-called cut-away must be used between the two scenes. In professional movie making this is referred to as "cutting away to a horse," a phrase which evolved during the making of all those Westerns where it was frequently necessary to change the screen direction of, say, a wagon train or a bunch of fast-riding Indians. By cutting away to a horse, this could then be accomplished.

CLOSE-UP—SIGNAL—Here we go in close on the signal and watch it change from go to stop. This is one of those "cutting away to a horse" shots. So far the train has been seen moving from left to right. In the next shot (which can be anywhere else on the layout) it is moving from right to left.

LONG SHOT—TRACK AND TRAIN—Here we have the train moving toward the camera and we keep the camera rolling from before the train enters the frame until after it has left the frame in order to give us an ample choice of possible places in which to cut to and from this scene. In order to make the next shot plausible, it is important that the audience is aware of the house which is located close to the track. Here we have a choice. If the house is on the side of the track away from the camera, then the shots which follow the one after this one, will have to have the train reverse screen-direction again. That is the way the script is written. On the other hand, if the house is located on the camera side of the track, meaning that it is in the foreground and we shoot past its back toward the moving train, then the train can continue to move from right to left in the following shots. (Placing the house in the foreground with its back walls to the camera has one advantage: It eliminates the need of having the window in the model house match the window to be used in the following scene.)

CLOSE SHOT—WINDOW OF HOUSE—Here we are cheating. We take a picture of the actual window of an actual house and use a real person in that window. That person's eyes should be giving the impression that he (she) is watching the train. In other words, if the house was located on the side of the track away from the camera, the eyes should be moving from camera-right to camera-left (the terms *camera-right* or *camera-left* mean the direction from the point of view of the camera. It is the opposite of stage directions used in the theatre, where one refers to *stage-right* and *stage-left*, meaning from the point of view of the actors and not the audience), but if the house was located on the same side of the track as the camera, then the person's eye should be moving from camera-left to camera-right. If there is no noticeable change in the kind of lighting used in this shot in relation to the preceding and following one, then this scene will look perfectly natural, and the audience should not be shocked by the sudden appearance of a real person. But keep it short. Staying on it too long may ruin the effect.

MEDIUM CLOSE SHOT—TRAIN—This is ostensibly shot from the point of view of the person sitting in the window in that house. The camera is at right angles to the track and we watch the train passing through the scene from either left to right (as in the script) or right to left, depending on where the house is located in relation to the track and the camera. It would be possible and possibly effective here to intercut. Scenes #13 and #14 two or three times in fairly quick succession. That is something that on can play with in the editing process.

LONG SHOT—TRACK AND TRAIN—Here the train is moving away from us continuing on its way. The screen direction here must coincide with the one used in Scene #14. It should be an angle shot, maybe at about 20 degrees or so to the track, and it is important that the audience is aware of the mountain range in the distance and of the fact that the track leads into a tunnel.

MEDIUM CLOSE SHOT—TRAIN—This shot, for all practical purposes, is a repeat of Scene #8, except that the background will have to be different, since we, by now, have traveled quie a few miles since leaving the freight yard. This and the following shots are again two of those "cutting away to a horse" situations, meaning that afterwards it makes no difference in which direction the train is traveling.

MEDIUM SHOT—ZOOM—TUNNEL—What we're trying to get here is the impression of moving toward the tunnel at the speed of the train. The effect will not be as realistic as we might like, because zooming in on a subject does not give the impression that the camera is moving toward the subject, but rather that the subject is moving toward the camera. To get the correct impression we would have to put the camera onto a dolly and move it along the track toward the tunnel while the film is rolling. But since this may prove impractical if not impossible, the zoom will have to do. The best solution is to use only a few frames of this scene in the final cut. If what we see of it passes quickly enough, we won't be too aware of the fact that the impression is somewhat phony.

CLOSE SHOT—TUNNEL ENTRANCE—Here we shoot the entrance to the tunnel at a 30- or 45-degree angle and let the train enter the scene (from either direction) and keep the camera rolling until the entire train has passed out of the frame.

CLOSE SHOT—TUNNEL ENTRANCE—We now place the camera onto the tracks and shoot straight into the tunnel, with the tunnel entrance filling most or all of the screen. We place the train in a position which puts the back of the caboose directly in front of the lens where it will be out of focus, blacking out virtually the entire picture. We now start the camera rolling and then start the train moving into the tunnel. We continue to keep the camera rolling until the last sign of the caboose has disappeared in the darkness of the tunnel.

With reference to the notation that the sound should turn hollow and then fade, here is one simple way to get that hollow reverberating sound. Get hold of a large wooden box, empty, and open on only one side. Place the tape player with the clickety-clack sound effects on a board, and place another tape-recorder next to it. Put that board outside the box and start both, the tape player and the tape recorder. Now slowly move the board with the player and recorder into the box as far as it will go. The deeper the box, the more reverberation effect will be achieved. Keep it running until you've recorded enough of it to be used in the scene in the picture. Fading the sound out can be done later on.

It may have already occurred to you that it may get a bit confusing later on when you've shot all those scenes and you're trying to figure out which scene goes where in the picture. This gets especially bad if you're working in 8-mm or super-8 motion picture film, which is so small that it is hard to tell what goes on in the film without projecting it.

"SLATE" EACH TAKE

For this reason it is definitely advisable to "slate" each take of each scene with numbers. (A *scene* is each individual setup. A *take* is each time that scene is shot. You may shoot a scene once, but decide that you could do better by having the train move faster or slower or by changing something else in that action or in the way the scene is lit. Thus you may end up with three, four or more takes of a given scene.) For this purpose you prepare yourself a small slate, any tablet or piece of cardboard covered with a sheet of clear plastic—in other words, anything that permits writing on it and then erasing it. Then use chalk or grease pencil and write on it: **SCENE 3, TAKE 2**, or whatever. Then, later on in your "cutting room," you don't have that difficulty in figuring out which piece of film is which. Remember that if you are making a five- or ten-minute film, if you do it right, you're likely to end up with several hundred scenes, many of them involving more than one take. Without having everything carefully slated, the resulting mess can be so bad that it might permanently discourage you from ever trying it again.

A DUPLICATE FILM

Depending on how interested you are in producing a film of lasting value, one that you, your family and your friends can enjoy in years to come, you may want to consider spending the extra money in having a separate print made of the final result. The right way to do this is to follow the method used by professional film makers. The film which you originally shot (I am assuming that everything is shot in color), once it has been processed, is referred to as the *original* and it should never be either projected or even run through a viewer. The reason is that projectors and viewers are likely to create some scratches on the film which can never be removed. Instead this original is sent to the nearest lab (there are such motion picture laboratories in New York, Chicago, Dallas, and, of course, Hollywood. Also, Eastman Kodak is equipped to duplicate the original). The lab makes a duplicate to you. The original is now kept in a cool place in its can, and remains untouched.

Edit the Workprint

The duplicate is what is known as the "workprint." This is what is now used to do all the editing. It can be projected or run through a viewer, and we don't care if it gets scratched up. Just be sure to keep the sprocket holes in descent shape, as torn sprockets can become annoying. Since we still have the original in its untouched condition, we can be fairly casual in experimenting with cutting the workprint. If the first cut we have made between two scenes doesn't seem to look quite right, we can change it, and if we find that we've lost a frame or two in the process, simply insert the appropriate number of frames in the form of leader, making a note with a grease pencil of the film, indicating where the final cut is supposed to take place.

Cut the Original

When the workprint has been edited to our complete satisfaction, we can project it and see what we've got. It's a good idea to run it many times to make sure that there are no annoying moments or cuts which don't work quite right. Then, when we know that we're fully satisfied, comes the job of cutting the original to match the workprint. **WEAR GLOVES!** All film editors wear thin white cloth gloves to make sure that they get no fingerprints on the film. Now the workprint is placed in a gimmick called a "synchronizer," which has several wheels with sprockets which turn at the same speed. The appropriate scene of the original is placed in the synchronizer next to the workprint, making sure that identical frames are in the identical position. This is best achieved by using the numbers which were printed by the manufacturer of the film on the edge of the original, and which were printed through when the workprint was made. They appear at one-foot intervals. We now cut and carefully splice the original to match the workprint. This has to be done with great care as one false cut can never be undone.

THE FINAL PRINT

When the original film has been cut to conform exactly to the workprint, it is again sent to the lab in order to once more be duplicated. The first such duplicate print of the edited original is referred to as the "first answerprint." Under normal conditions this first print will be the only one you'll ever have made, and it can now be projected over and over again. But remember, you still have the original in its pristine condition. So, if anything ever happens to your print, such as it tears or sprocket holes get ruined or whatever, you can always have another answer print made by the lab.

Aside from protecting your work in the form of the carefully preserved original, this method also has the advantage that the final film is likely to give you less trouble in projection than would any film that has dozens if not hundreds of splices in it. Splices, no matter how carefully they are made, have an unpleasant habit of coming apart after repeated runs through a projector. And, if you use your edited original for projection and something like that happens, you're out of luck for good.

MAKE A STORYBOARD

Many professional film makers, in addition to a detailed shooting script, prepare a visual blueprint of the proposed picture, referred to as a "storyboard." A storyboard is simply a sequence of sketches, often quite primitive, which give an impression of what each scene is to look like. Such a story board can be very helpful in visualizing what we have in mind. No talent for drawing or sketching is necessary. Very simple drawings are all that is needed. I, myself, can't draw my way out of a paper bag, but with whatever limited talent I have in that direction, I prepared such a storyboard for the sample sequence described in the shooting script (Fig. 13-1). It's very primitive, but it does give a visual impression of what the film will eventually look like. Anyone, especially those who are inexperienced in working in the motion picture medium, might be well advised to prepare such a storyboard before embarking on a more ambitious project.

Index

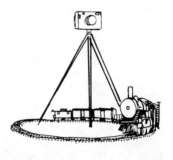

176